P9-BBV-373

# FATHER-SON HEALING
## •An Adult Son's Guide•

### JOSEPH ILARDO, PH.D.

*NEW HARBINGER PUBLICATIONS, INC.*

## Publisher's Note

This publication is designed to provide accurate and authoritative information in regard to the subject matter covered. It is sold with the understanding that the publisher is not engaged in rendering psychological, financial, legal, or other professional services. If expert assistance or counseling is needed, the services of a competent professional should be sought.

Copyright © Joseph A. Ilardo
          New Harbinger Publications, Inc.
          5674 Shattuck Avenue
          Oakland, CA 94609

Library of Congress Catalog Card Number: 93-084711
ISBN 1-879237-47-4 paperback
ISBN 1-879237-48-2 hardcover

All rights reserved.
Printed in the United States of America on recycled paper.
Cover design by SHELBY DESIGNS & ILLUSTRATES

1st Printing 1993, 5,000 copies

To my father and all the men whose lives go unheralded, but who—in their quiet, unpretentious ways—have made it possible for a lesser man to put in print their wisdom, courage, and love.

# Contents

# Acknowledgments

I want to thank the many people who have had a part in the preparation of this book. To my students and colleagues at Herbert Lehman College of the City University of New York, who have been generous in providing ideas and stimulation, thank you. I am especially grateful to Professor Albert Bermel, who was kind enough to read sections of the manuscript and offer valuable suggestions. To the many fathers and sons who shared your stories—and in many cases, your grief—with me, your contributions have been invaluable. My wife, Roberta, and my daughters, Janine and Karen Leigh, have supported me in every imaginable way during the course of my writing. Without their part in the creation of this book, it would not have been completed. I want to thank Patrick Fanning and Matthew McKay for their enthusiasm and wisdom as this project unfolded. Finally, I want to thank my editor, Barbara Quick, not only for her professionalism, but for her many thoughtful and valuable comments, suggestions, and challenges. Her astuteness has improved the book immeasurably.

# 1

# Fathers and Sons

When Tim learned that his wife was pregnant, he was delighted. Married for three years, he and Jane had been trying to conceive for several months. Jane's pregnancy proceeded smoothly. Both she and Tim anticipated the birth of their child with genuine eagerness. Tim took pride in painting the baby's room and building a cradle. Jane chose curtains and decorated the room with great care. Together, and with the help of Jane's friends at a baby shower, the couple assembled everything their child would need, from equipment to clothes. All was ready for the child's arrival.

Jane delivered a healthy seven-pound, three-ounce son. Both husband and wife looked forward to taking the child home and feeling for the first time like a family.

The earliest days were a blur of emotion and activity. Euphoric but exhausted, and a little frightened of her new responsibilities, Jane set about learning how to be a mother. Keeping her baby fed and happy suddenly took all her time. But Tim was an excellent helpmate, cooking, shopping, and doing the housework that Jane couldn't keep up with now. Sleep was a problem for both of them, as their infant son's demands didn't follow any sort of schedule; but the love they felt for him made every expenditure of time and effort seem more than worthwhile.

Jane and Tim had rarely felt closer than they did during the earliest weeks following the birth of their son. As time passed, though, a subtle and disturbing change came about. The more Jane threw herself into the myriad responsibilities of child-care, the more Tim began to feel just slightly resentful. It was clear that his wife's highest priority was now their child. Of course Tim accepted this; he saw it as appropriate, and a clear indication that Jane would be an excellent mother. Yet a sense of exclusion and loss began gnawing at him.

Jane had no time for Tim anymore. When Tim came home from work, Jane treated him like he was "on duty." When they fell into bed at the end of the evening, all Jane wanted to do was sleep. Tim decided that it might be best to step aside: it seemed absurd to enter into competition for his wife's attention.

Tim reacted by spending more time at work than was necessary. His initial eagerness to help out at home began to wane. His role, after all, was that of provider. He had begun to grow tired of playing house, anyway.

Jane couldn't fail to notice the change in her husband's attitude. She had appreciated all the help he'd given her, and wondered now whether she'd neglected to tell him so. But she herself felt that her resources were being taxed to the limit: did she need to baby Tim and her baby, too? Couldn't Tim see that she needed to be loved and cared for and appreciated as well? She kept her thoughts to herself, though, reasoning that, as a new father, Tim was likely to go through a period of adjustment. After all, the demands of fatherhood were new to him.

Then everything exploded one night, when Jane had gone to great effort to prepare dinner to celebrate the baby's two-month-old birthday. Even though Jane had told him she'd be cooking something special, Tim failed to return from work when he said he would. The meal was all but ruined—and Jane was famished—by the time he arrived. Confronting him, Jane tried to explain through her tears why she was so upset. But instead of being understanding, Tim acted angry and defensive. He accused his wife of devoting all her waking hours to the child, and trying to "fit him in" as an afterthought. He resented it, he said, and found being a father a lot less fun than he'd expected. She asked him how he thought *she* felt, stuck in the house all day with a baby who refused to take naps and required her attention round the clock.

Following their argument, both Tim and Jane felt guilty and confused. Surely this turn of events was something that neither of them had expected.

As most parents will testify, the experience of Jane and Tim is not terribly unusual. The problem that arose between them is predictable, rooted in the differing needs and roles of fathers and mothers after the birth of a child. I've told this story here to illustrate some of the reasons why the relationship between fathers and sons gets off to a rocky start.

If your relationship with your own father is less than satisfactory, the chances are good that the problem can be traced back to the earliest weeks and months of your life. Your own father's experience may well have been much like Tim's, as he struggled to come to terms with your birth and adjust to its effects on his relationship with your mother. Even if you were not a firstborn child, the same forces operated: your father had to redefine his relationship with his wife and adjust psychologically to the many changes each birth demanded.

Unfortunately, the tie between fathers and sons doesn't only start off badly; it often remains problematical throughout much of their lives. The reasons are biological, cultural, social, and psychological. All four factors influence the kinds of relationships established by fathers and sons.

By the time you're done reading this chapter, you'll see why it's no surprise if you and your father experience each other as difficult and unfathomable, and your relationship is a source of pain, disillusionment, and disappointment.

## The Impact of Biological Factors on Fathers and Sons

Both your parents participated in your conception. But once you were born, your father was relegated to a position outside the intense bond tying you to your mother. This is as nature dictates.

The intensity of the mother-son tie is rooted in biology. It is the mother who bears and gives birth to the child. From the earliest moments of his extra-uterine existence, the son recognizes his mother's voice and quickly comes to know her in terms of all the other senses—touch, taste, sight, and smell. Nothing is more intimate than the mother-child bond. In most situations, mother is synonymous with comfort and security. She is the source of food and, indeed, of life itself.

Mother and son satisfy each other's needs on a purely biological level. His sucking instinct drives the production of milk in her breasts in a perfect supply-and-demand system. His need for care complements her need to nurture.

Mother is equipped biologically and trained socially to be the child's primary caretaker. Her overwhelming presence largely defines the child's world. Intimate, daily contact establishes the intense and all-absorbing relationship between a mother and her infant. If there were no substitute mother to step in, the mother's death would likely mean the child's death as well.

During the earliest weeks of life, a father can never be as close to his child as the mother. Shared genes aside, no biological factors connect father and son. In fact, at the moment his sperm fertilizes the woman's egg, father's strictly biological role is over. The father can leave after the moment of conception without compromising the child's physical survival—although the father's absence can and does have profound psychological repercussions.

## Men Who Nurture

Research reported by psychiatrist Kyle Pruett reveals wide variations among individual males in terms of their temperamental suitability for nurturing. He lists a number of factors that enter into a man's willingness to nurture a child:

- Social conditioning plays a major role in shaping how comfortable a man will be in that capacity. If the particular social environment in which the man was raised devalues childcare and disparages it as "women's work," then the man is unlikely to show much interest in participating.

- A man's previous experience with children has an impact. If he was an older sibling charged with the care of younger ones, he's likely to be more comfortable in the role of caretaker.

- A man's age at the time of his son's birth is important. Younger men, unburdened by such concerns as their health and that of their aging parents, are typically freer to be more actively involved in the day-to-day care of their offspring than older men.

- First-time fathers typically show more interest in being involved with their issue than men who have fathered many children.

- Finally, the birth-order of the child makes a difference: fathers are typically more involved with firstborn children (regardless of gender) than with those born later.

All these factors aside, there is yet another biological barrier to intimacy between you and your father: the two of you have simply never been—and can never be—in sync. You can never be peers because of the age difference between you. While you and your mother were likely able to bridge the "age gap" because your needs were complementary, no such mutuality of interest has worked in favor of you and your father.

Your father's concerns, interests, and emotional needs have never been the same as yours. The two of you are perpetually at different points in the male life cycle. Your needs and concerns can never parallel his, nor can they be complementary for very long, because each of you is always at a place far removed from the other as he makes his way through the life cycle.

Berkeley sociologist Claude Fischer asked a sample of adults whom they turn to when they need to talk about personal matters, or need an opinion they value. Though all the adult males surveyed had adult sons, not one father in the sample felt close enough to his son to consider him as a confidant. (Clinical experience suggests that sons are at least as likely to avoid turning to their fathers.)

Consider the following sketch. A man—call him Robert—marries at age 28. Five years later, his wife becomes pregnant. His first child, a son, is born when Robert is 33. At this point in his life, the young father is deeply involved in building a career. Though he loves his wife and son, Robert's energies are focused largely on work. His parents are beginning to get on in years, and he is concerned about visiting and helping them out around the house when he can. He is also concerned about his physical health. He reads and hears a great deal about fitness and is conscientious about running and exercising regularly. In an attempt to combine his efforts to remain healthy with his hobbies and interests, he has joined a men's softball league; he also plays tennis with a partner on weekends.

Five years later, Robert's son is starting school. The child's needs are for play and instruction. He wants to spend time with his dad. He needs to learn about the world, to socialize with peers, and to manage school responsibilities. Robert, meantime, is now 38. When his company was taken over the year before, he lost his job. Although he quickly found another, he must now prove his worth to his new employer. Robert's responsibilities make it necessary for him to spend long hours at work. He must manage his career, tend to his wife's needs and to those of his mother now that his father has died.

The needs of father and son are sadly out of sync. For as long as both of them live, they will always be at very different points in the life cycle. It's true that their interests and needs overlap at times. For example, Robert's interest in baseball dovetails nicely with his son's enthusiasm for the sport. In the main, however, the two live in quite separate worlds. Throughout their lives, fathers and sons experience a perpetual asynchronicity.

Given the fundamental biological distance between fathers and sons, it's not surprising that for many sons, their father is loved and admired, but also frightening, unfathomable, distant, and a source of confusion. These feelings are heightened by cultural factors that contribute to the distancing of father and son.

The following exercise can help you personalize the issues just discussed.

## Exercise
### *Looking Backwards*

Take some time to answer the five questions below as they relate to your early childhood, pre-adolescence, adolescence, young adulthood, and middle age. There's one form provided for each time period.

## *Looking Backwards: Early Childhood (Birth–6 years)*

1. What did my father and I do together during this period?
   _____

   What did we talk about or share? _____

   What are my best memories of this period?_____

   My worst memories? _____

   How do I remember thinking and feeling about my father
   during this period? _____

   How do I suppose he thought and felt about me? (If possible, ask him.)_____
   _____

2. What conflicts characterized our relationship during this
   period? _____
   _____

   How did we negotiate them?_____

3. How did my father change (or seem to change) during
   this period? _____
   _____

4. How did my emotional attachment to my father change
   during this period? _____

   In what ways did changes in my thinking and behavior
   seem to affect him and our relationship? _____
   _____

5. What feelings, extrafamilial concerns, or needs affected my
   father during this period? _____

   Did he show them? If so, in what ways (or in what ways
   did he use to avoid them)?_____

## *Looking Backwards: Pre-Adolescence (6–12 years)*

1. What did my father and I do together during this period? _____

   What did we talk about or share? _____

   What are my best memories of this period?_____

   My worst memories? _____

   How do I remember thinking and feeling about my father during this period? _____

   How do I suppose he thought and felt about me? (If possible, ask him.)_____

2. What conflicts characterized our relationship during this period? _____
   How did we negotiate them?_____

3. How did my father change (or seem to) during this period? _____
   Did he seem to think or behave differently from the way he did before? How did that affect me and our relationship? _____

4. How did my emotional attachment to my father change during this period? _____
   In what ways did changes in my thinking and behavior seem to affect him and our relationship? _____

5. What feelings, extrafamilial concerns, or needs affected my father during this period? _____
   Did he show them? If so, in what ways (or in what ways did he use to avoid them)?_____

### *Looking Backwards: Adolescence* (12–18 *years*)

1. What did my father and I do together during this period? _____

   What did we talk about or share? _____

   What are my best memories of this period?_____

   My worst memories? _____

   How do I remember thinking and feeling about my father during this period? _____

   How do I suppose he thought and felt about me? (If possible, ask him.)_____

   _____

2. What conflicts characterized our relationship during this period? _____

   How did we negotiate them?_____

   _____

3. How did my father change (or seem to) during this period? _____

   Did he seem to think or behave differently from the way he did before? How did that affect me and our relationship? _____

4. How did my emotional attachment to my father change during this period? _____

   In what ways did changes in my thinking and behavior seem to affect him and our relationship? _____

   _____

5. What feelings, extrafamilial concerns, or needs affected my father during this period? _____

   Did he show them? If so, in what ways (or in what ways did he use to avoid them)?_____

## *Looking Backwards: Young Adulthood* (18–40 years)

1. What did my father and I do together during this period?
_____

   What did we talk about or share? _____
_____

   What are my best memories of this period?_____
_____

   My worst memories? _____
_____

   How do I remember thinking and feeling about my father during this period? _____
_____

   How do I suppose he thought and felt about me? (If possible, ask him.)_____
_____

2. What conflicts characterized our relationship during this period? _____
   How did we negotiate them?_____

3. How did my father change (or seem to) during this period? _____
   Did he seem to think or behave differently from the way he did before? How did that affect me and our relationship? _____

4. How did my emotional attachment to my father change during this period? _____
_____

   In what ways did changes in my thinking and behavior seem to affect him and our relationship? _____
_____

5. What feelings, extrafamilial concerns, or needs affected my father during this period? _____
   Did he show them? If so, in what ways (or in what ways did he use to avoid them)?_____

### *Looking Backwards: Middle Age (40 years plus)*

1. What did my father and I do together during this period?
   _____

   What did we talk about or share? _____

   _____

   What are my best memories of this period?_____

   _____

   My worst memories? _____

   _____

   How do I remember thinking and feeling about my father
   during this period? _____
   How do I suppose he thought and felt about me? (If possible, ask him.)_____

   _____

2. What conflicts characterized our relationship during this
   period? _____
   How did we negotiate them?_____

3. How did my father change (or seem to) during this
   period? _____
   Did he seem to think or behave differently from the way
   he did before? How did that affect me and our relationship? _____

4. How did my emotional attachment change during this
   period? _____

   _____

   In what ways did changes in my thinking and behavior
   seem to affect him and our relationship? _____

   _____

5. What feelings, extrafamilial concerns, or needs affected my
   father during this period? _____
   Did he show them? If so, in what ways (or in what ways
   did he use to avoid them)?_____

# The Impact of Cultural Factors on Fathers and Sons

Becoming a father is the cultural and biological confirmation of a man's masculinity. In many cultures, the epitome of "maleness" is achieved by fathering one or more sons. It's not surprising that years of cultural training come to a head as a man responds to the expectations associated with the role of father—especially the role of father to a boy.

In every culture, males are conditioned to behave in distinctive ways that set them apart from females, inculcated to think, feel, and behave according to particular social norms. What men learn not to do, no less than what they learn to do, affects the relationships between fathers and sons profoundly.

Here's a quick activity designed to heighten your awareness of the kinds of cultural conditioning men receive in our society. Read each trait in the list below, and decide whether the trait is typical of males (that is, one usually considered masculine or one which men are likely to display) or females. Mark each box with an M or F.

- [ ] Keeps his or her emotions under control
- [ ] Stays cool under pressure
- [ ] Is emotionally expressive
- [ ] Is logical and cold
- [ ] Is empathic and warm
- [ ] Is the strong, silent type
- [ ] Is able to ask for help
- [ ] Behaves as though invulnerable
- [ ] Tends to be isolated emotionally
- [ ] Is uncomfortable in moments of emotionally vulnerability

You most likely marked each box according to the norms of the culture in which you grew up. Although variations in answers exist because of the unique experience of each person, it's likely that you (if you're a native-born American) answered all but the third, fifth, and seventh items with an M, and the other three items with an F. Your answers reflect the biases imposed on males and females by our culture.

Long before they become fathers, men (and women, too) learn gender-based ways of thinking, feeling, and behaving. For example, men learn to be tough, to compete, ignore their own pain and perform. They learn that to be a man, they must put aside imagination, tenderness, and vulnerability. Such traits are for children. Perhaps those qualities have a place in the lives of women, but they certainly are not consistent with manhood. Men are conditioned to ignore their emotional inner life and are rewarded instead for developing an abstract, objective, and impersonal style. As a result, they are not prepared to talk about their own inner lives or the inner lives of their sons. Never having learned to nurture themselves emotionally, they are ill-prepared to provide emotional nurturance for their sons. Because they have learned that to express tenderness is feminine, they don't know how to be tender to their sons. Little wonder that sons find fathers so out of touch with the really important concerns of childhood.

Traditionally in our culture, men have learned the specifics of fathering by observing their own father, and absorbing father stereotypes from literature and the media. From such sources, men have learned that their job as a father is to provide and protect. Their success has been tied to their ability to stand apart from the emotional bond between mother and son, while ensuring their safety, and seeing to it that their physical needs are met.

Given these parameters and this conditioning, it should not be surprising that a good many men redouble their commitment to work after a son is born. There are four reasons for this, as the story that opened this chapter illustrates. They are:

- The work world is masculine, whereas home and hearth are feminine

- Work is a way of reducing the provider anxiety sparked by a child's birth

- On the job, a man knows what's expected (he may have no such clear understanding of the role expectations associated with being a father)

- In the workplace, a man can constructively vent his anger at having been abandoned by his wife while simultaneously avoiding the burdens and demands of a wife and child

Let's look more closely at each of these.

For some new fathers, spending time at home seems to undermine their masculinity. To a typical American man raised in the 1960s or earlier, the work world is the masculine world, whereas involvement with the family may feel like part of the feminine realm. Our society has offered fewer rewards for being a nurturing father than for being a hard-working and unemotional provider and employee.

Other men, upon becoming fathers, feel more keenly than ever the burdens of providing. They feel compelled to invest themselves in work, since this is consistent with their culturally prescribed role, as well as helping them manage what has been called *provider anxiety.*

Becoming a father can pose a problem when men lack a model of how to behave as a man in a family. (Current data reported by Keen and Corneau indicate that single-parent families, approximately 89 percent of which are headed by women, raise 50 percent of today's children. Even in intact families, the father may well be physically absent much of the time because of the demands of work. He may be emotionally removed because of his upbringing and personal limitations.) Men who lack models of how to be a father are uncomfortable with the role. Escaping to the workplace or some other traditionally masculine realm where expectations are familiar is both safe and consistent with cultural expectations.

The places men go to avoid the burdens and uncertainties of fathering are almost limitless in number. Socioeconomic class, ethnicity, interests, and the physical proximity of available escapes are four of the key variables that determine their choices. Some men take up hunting, spending many days away from home during the season and many months between seasons preparing for the hunt. Others become regulars at the pool hall or local bar. Professionals may pass their Saturdays playing golf with their associates. In the life of one man I know, professional athletics has become a central organizing theme for his escapes from home life. He has season tickets for his city's football, basketball, and hockey teams, and attends all the games.

Finally, psychological factors may propel a father out of the home. Work provides an outlet for the anger and aggression that may result from the husband feeling abandoned by his wife as she nurtures their child. He may leave to escape feelings of intense emotional neediness. The workplace may represent a safe haven from a home dominated by a demanding child and the needs of an exhausted wife.

## The Impact of Social Factors on Fathers and Sons

Before the Industrial Revolution, fathers were often available to answer questions, provide instruction, and serve as a constant model for their sons. As fathers began to leave home early in the day to work in factories, they were absent for most of a child's waking hours, and usually returned home tired and emotionally unavailable.

Of course, it would be silly to idealize fathering prior to the Industrial Revolution. Fathers then were no better at fathering than men are today. In many ways, they were no doubt more brutal and far less attuned to the needs of their sons. Nevertheless, they were around to be observed, and to some degree understood, if only by virtue of their proximity.

Since the Industrial Revolution, father has become a mysterious figure to many sons. Where did he go during the day? What did he do? What was his life apart from the family?

More recently, a number of major social changes have also had a profound influence on the relationships between fathers and sons. The three I will focus on here are the prevalence of divorce, the increasing presence of women in the workforce, and the emphasis on independence in the cultural conditioning of contemporary males.

## Divorce

The statistics, though familiar, are still staggering: 60 percent of children born in 1987 will not be living with or supported by their birth father by the time they reach adolescence. Single-parent families, approximately 89 percent of which are headed by the mother, and from which the father is absent, raise the majority of today's children.

This means that more than half of all sons born to contemporary couples will not have the experience of living with their biological father for a significant portion of their lives. Some will never even know their fathers. Many others will have only the most distant relationship with him. (All too often, a few years after the divorce, noncustodial fathers begin skipping visitation; shortly thereafter, they begin withholding childcare payments: thus, *Newsweek* recently reported that according to a 1990 U.S. Census Bureau study, of the five million women who are supposed to receive child-support payments, only 50 percent reported receiving all that was due them; 25 percent received nothing at all.)

These boys may resent their father's failure to provide child-support, and may even be able to get in touch with their anger at their fathers. But they rarely appreciate the significance of what they're not getting by virtue of their father's absence.

It's clear, however, that they miss out on a great deal, and that their lives are profoundly damaged by that lack. More will be said about this later in the book.

Before moving on, one last point needs to be made. Fathers who fail to maintain relationships with their children suffer a great deal themselves. According to one expert, noncustodial fathers experience problems ranging from depression and shame to abnormally high levels of chemical addictions and physical illnesses. Theirs is a story almost as unhappy as that of their offspring.

## Working Mothers

The changes in family life occasioned by women returning to work are significant. For many men, their wife's absence from the home triggers confusion and resentment. Even those men who welcome the added income and the reduction of pressure on themselves may be left adrift by their wife's career. Asked to play a meaningful role in childcare and home management, they are often unprepared for both. They may feel overwhelmed, inadequate, and lost.

As a result, some men may withdraw or leave rather than admit they can't handle the dual responsibilities of provider and assistant homemaker. Others may initially welcome childcare responsibilities, but eventually come to resent the burdens it imposes. The son (or daughter) may bear the brunt of the father's confusion, anger, and feelings of inadequacy.

## The Ethic of Independence

Another social trend encourages men to "go it alone." In the popular culture, men are traditionally portrayed as strong, independent, and emotionally unconnected. (Think of the type of characters portrayed by John Wayne, Sean Connery, and others.) Accepting this view of manhood further contributes to the isolation of contemporary men—at least in industrialized, Western nations, and the United States in particular. By extension, the ethic of independence contributes to the distancing of fathers and sons.

This phenomenon is multifaceted. A man subscribes to it when he places a very high value on outward achievement and accomplishment. Hard work, even work that borders on the compulsive, is rewarded, sometimes quite generously. As a result, men learn to be resolute and deeply committed to proving their personal worth—and their value as providers—through long hours and fanatical commitment to the job. Many corporations encourage employees to affiliate and identify with the company as a substitute family. This forced and artificial intimacy creates the illusion of emotional satisfaction, drawing the employee further away from his own biological family.

The following questions can help you discern whether your father achieved his sense of worth and identity from his work, and whether work became an addiction in his life. (In addition to answering these questions from your father's perspective, try answering them from your own. Do you feel, think, or behave as described?)

## *Work Inventory*

| | Yes | No |
|---|---|---|
| Did work provide your father with more excitement and satisfaction than his family or other involvements and activities? | | |
| Did he have trouble leaving his work in the office, and instead bring it home in the evenings and on the weekends, and when the family went on vacation? | | |
| Did he regularly work more than 40 hours per week? | | |
| Did he assume responsibility for jobs that weren't his because he was afraid that the work wouldn't get done otherwise? | | |
| Did his long hours hurt your family or have an adverse impact on other relationships that were important to him? | | |
| Did he turn his hobbies and interests into money-making ventures? | | |
| Did he get impatient with people who had priorities other than work? | | |
| Did he worry about being a failure even when things were going well? | | |
| Did he get irritated when your mother or other people urged him to ease up on work and start doing other things? | | |
| Did he seem to think about work much or most of the time? | | |

If you answered yes to more than two questions, chances are that your father subscribed to the ethic of independence when it came to work. In fact, work may have been a real problem for him. (If you would answer similarly, the chances are good that the same is true of you.)

Another indication that a man has bought into the ethic of independence is revealed by his orientation toward himself. He may, for example, commit himself to a rigid workout schedule. Health, fitness, and exercise may take much of his otherwise free time. The family thus places a distant third, behind work and an interest in maintaining his physical well-being.

Abraham Maslow's popular model shows a person's needs arranged in a hierarchy, like a pyramid, with physiological needs at the bottom and self-realization needs at the top. Widely taught in psychology courses, this model reflects the same ethic of independence. Maslow is typical of male psychologists in emphasizing self-realization. His view of life's task leads to an emphasis on power, control, dominance, isolation, and alienation from others. Thus, even supposedly objective psychology falls victim to a way of looking at life that encourages people to "go it alone."

# The Impact of Psychological Factors on Fathers and Sons

Psychological factors can also contribute to the problematical nature of your relationship with your father. Of the two I will discuss, it's safe to say that both are unspoken, and perhaps unconscious, in your father's experience. They both nevertheless have shaped his responses to you.

First, a father may feel quite ambivalent about the birth of a son. After all, the son confirms the father's mortality, representing the next replacement generation of males. If life events proceed as expected, he will outlive and supercede the father. It's usually recognized by the father that his son will outdo him in many ways. As life progresses, the son may well be the better educated and wealthier of the two. He is bound to be more comfortable with technological advances that may remain a mystery to his father. As the boy reaches manhood, he probably will be attractive to women who have no sexual interest in the father. And so on.

Second, the birth of a son may trigger reactions that impede the father's ability to comfortably assume the role of nurturing male. For example, as the story of Tim and Jane showed, the father may experience intense emotional neediness when he watches his wife nurture their son. He may also resent the son, whose arrival has resulted in his wife's abandoning him and focusing much, if not all, of her love and attention on the child. Again, the son's unceasing demands and the wife's neediness (she may be physically depleted and overwhelmed by the burdens of motherhood) may trigger anger and resentment.

## To Summarize

You now know some of the biological, cultural, social, and psychological reasons why the relationships between fathers and sons are so often problematical, disappointing, and confusing. In later chapters, you'll learn more about these and other factors, and will come to appreciate their far-ranging implications.

## Recommended Reading

Anderson, C. (1983) *Father: The Figure and the Force*. New York: Warner Books.

Appleton, W. S. (1984) *Fathers and Daughters*. New York: Berkeley Books.

Corneau, G. (1991) *Absent Fathers, Lost Sons*. Boston: Shambhala.

Hardy, M., and J. Hough. (1991) *Against the Wall: Men's Reality in a Codependent Culture*. New York: Ballantine Books.

Keen, S. (1991) *Fire in the Belly: On Being a Man*. New York: Bantam Books.

Klein, B. (May-June 1985) "Fathering: The First Time," *Social Work*, vol. 3, no. 30, 264-67.

Lamb, M. (October 1982) "Why Swedish Fathers Aren't Liberated," *Psychology Today*, 74-77.

Levinson, D. J. (1978) *The Seasons of a Man's Life*. New York: Ballantine Books.

Lidz, T. (1968) *The Person: His Development Throughout the Life Cycle*. New York: Basic Books.

Miller, S. (1983) *Men and Friendship*. Los Angeles: Jeremey P. Tarcher, Inc.

Osherson, S. (1986) *Finding Our Fathers: How a Man's Life Is Shaped by his Relationship With His Father*. New York: Fawcett-Columbine.

Pruett, K. (1987) *The Nurturing Father: Journey Toward the Complete Man*. New York: Warner Books.

# 2

# Father's Influence

It's hardly news to state that your father exerted a tremendous influence on your personality and outlook on life. His role in shaping you has been unique and irreplaceable. In this chapter you'll learn first about the traditional view of a father's role and influence. You'll also learn about some of the many specific life skills and attitudes he likely taught you. Finally, you'll learn about your father's impact on your self-esteem. This, in fact, is the main thrust of this chapter: not only will you see why and how your father influenced your self-esteem; you'll also come to recognize the likely long-term effects of that influence, for both good and ill, on your life.

# The Traditional View of Father's Influence

From the perspective of traditional psychology, your father served two key functions in your life. As the first "significant other" in your experience, he served as a sort of introduction to the world apart from your mother. As the first male with whom you had contact, he shaped your sexual identity.

## Your First Significant Other

It would be difficult to overestimate the intensity of the mother-son tie. During the earliest days and weeks of life, mother is the source of virtually everything the child needs: food, comfort, tenderness, and care. So far as the newborn is concerned, there is only mother. The lines between him and her are blurred during the earliest weeks of life: he does not know where he ends and she begins. Over time, of course, the child begins to distinguish between self and mother. According to psychiatrists, father lays no small role in the child's making this distinction. Father reduces the intensity of the mother-son bond. He literally and figuratively comes between the two of them. To the child, father is a stranger. He looks, smells, and feels different from mother. He is novel, interesting, and—just by virtue of his presence in the child's very narrow world—extremely important. Father forces the son to recognize that there's more to the world than mother.

At the same time, father implants the idea that the child is a being who is different from mother, that he has an existence apart from her. The very fundamental notion of personhood is the product of father's presence. He imparts a silent message: "You are someone other than mother; you are a person in your own right. You and I have a relationship apart from yours with mother." This message can hardly be more critical in the development of the child's sense of himself as an independent person.

Another consequence follows from father's being the child's first significant other. By his comings and goings, father imparts important information about separations. The child gradually comes to realize that someone's leaving, even for extended periods (measured in hours, and perhaps even days) doesn't imply that the person is gone forever. From the child's perspective, it's possible for father to leave the scene for long periods of time and still return. This contributes to the child's faith in the permanence of objects in his world. At some point, it undoubtedly also contributes to the development of curiosity. After all, if father isn't with me during these extended absences, where is he? Father serves as an indicator that there is a broader world apart from the child's. (Of course, if a mother works outside the home, the child also learns this message from her.)

Finally, father provides a point of reference for the son. Mother may be more attuned to the son's needs: she likely understands his cries, knows when he is uncomfortable or hungry, senses when he is frightened or ill. Father, less attuned and less sensitively aware, is also less pliable. He is probably a less responsive individual—a sort of constant against which the son can sense himself. This function of the father is more clearly evident when the son is older, when he tests himself against father both physically and emotionally. For example, when the boy is a toddler, father and son may wrestle playfully. The son measures his strength by the success or failure of his efforts to defeat father. During the son's adolescence, he may test his courage and determination even more directly and realistically as he makes requests (or demands) of father, and occasionally defies him.

## Father Shaped Your Sexual Identity

Sex and gender are not equivalent. A child's sex is determined by the genitalia. Gender, however, is a cultural construct that goes far beyond sexual organs. *Maleness* is a set of beliefs, attitudes, and behaviors that are considered appropriate for males in a specific culture. Father's role in helping the son establish a firm sexual identity as a male is crucially important. He teaches the son what it means to be a man, since he serves as the vehicle by which his culture's view of masculinity is conveyed to the boy.

Father prepares the son to conform to society's norms of male behavior. For example, he will treat boys and girls differently. (Mothers do, too, but they make less of a distinction, especially during the earliest months of life.) Boys are roughhoused more. They are likely to be described as "strong," "big," and "brave," whereas girls are more likely to be described as "sweet," "cuddly," and "cute." Father will also model male behavior, teaching by example how men think and behave. Thousands of little and seemingly trivial incidents, all carefully observed and taken in by the son, contribute to his establishing a male sexual identity.

## Exercise
### Gender Modeling

Think back on your childhood, recalling some of the differences in each of the following:

- The way mother spoke with and handled you; the way father did
- The terms and labels assigned to you by mother and father
- Mother's expectations of you versus father's
- How you felt about mother and father

Use extra paper to write down your recollections.

# Father as a Teacher of Skills and Attitudes

To survive and win acceptance as a male, you've had to learn a laundry list of life skills and attitudes. Many of these, as will soon become evident, are extensions of the just-described concept of sexual identity. Your father played a crucial role in teaching them.

In this section of the chapter, I will enumerate several of the more important skills a father teaches. In the course of this discussion, I will make no judgments about whether the skills taught are desirable. In some cases, it could be argued that they are not. My purpose, however, is not to provide a critique of our society. Nor is it to revise current thinking about what it means (or ought to mean) to be a man or woman. Rather, my intent is simply to describe as accurately as I can the skills that a father usually teaches his son.

## Society's Expectations

As a child, you had to learn to meet society's expectations of a man.

*A man must be able to compete.* Fathers teach competitiveness. They encourage sons to compete, to learn how to strategize. Boys are exposed to the world of competition early—through sports, for example. (Girls are increasingly being primed to be physically competitive as well.)

*A man must learn to formulate and pursue goals.* Fathers convey the importance of achieving goals by having goal-oriented expectations for their son. Whereas mothers may feel that it's enough for a child simply to play, or to create in a vague and ill-defined way, father will convey the message that play activities should have significance or be leading somewhere. "What are you doing?" father will ask. "Why?" Or again, "What is that a drawing of?"

Along these lines, I recall an experience I had as a high school student. I'd been studying elementary physics and had been exposed to the definition of a *machine*, a device that does work. I found a small electric motor in our basement, and managed to rig up a sort of primitive motorized pulley. Proud of my accomplishment (though my machine served no useful purpose), I showed it to my father. He was a mechanically inclined man who, I thought, would appreciate my device. He watched the machine hum for a few moments, then turned to me and dismissed it with a simple observation: "It doesn't do anything!" Though I was crushed by his failure to appreciate my achievement, I learned a lesson: whatever I did had to serve some purpose if it was going to impress Dad!

*A man must have discipline in order to succeed in the face of challenges and dangers, and to see tasks through.* Whereas mothers are typically understanding, tolerant, and forgiving in the face of a son's lack of discipline (at least during the child's youngest years), fathers play quite a different role. Many fathers consider it their job to impart a sense of discipline to their child. They may do so by imposing punishments or withholding approval. They may discipline themselves. Sometimes fathers are accused of being unduly harsh in disciplining their sons, and indeed some are; but it is undoubtedly true that to a great degree it falls on them (if they are present in the household) to teach the all-important skill of self-discipline to their sons.

*A man must learn how to deal with failure and disappointment.* Fathers realize that their sons won't succeed at everything. When a son fails, a father conveys by his manner and words how best to deal with failure. He also conveys this message by the way he deals with his own failures.

*A man must learn to make sacrifices and suffer in silence.* Fathers teach sons that a real man must be able to forego the satisfaction of his own needs without complaining in order to serve the greater good. He may do so with such admonishments as, "Don't be a baby!" and "Be a big boy!" He may do so by modeling sacrifice himself, or by suffering silently when he is ill or hurt emotionally. In these and other ways, the son learns that men are tough and can put up with pain and disappointments. Indeed, he likely learns that the ability to suffer in silence is a measure of his manhood.

Many other skills could be identified. The point, however, is clear: father has a critical function to play in teaching skills a son needs to survive in the world.

## How To Deal With Aggression and Authority

You had to learn appropriate male behaviors, attitudes, pastimes, and socially acceptable outlets for male aggressiveness as a child.

*A man must learn to participate in and enjoy typical male activities.* One friend of mine is the father of a boy and a girl, both under nine. He regularly takes his son to the batting range, where he can learn to hit balls. (He takes his daughter to her gymnastics lesson on another day of the week.) This behavior is typical of conscientious fathers who work hard to prepare their sons for the activities in which they will be expected to participate as they grow older. Men also model how to be "the man around the house." They do repairs, participate in the shopping, and perhaps do some of the traditionally male household chores as well (such as take out the garbage or mow the lawn). Fathers will often invite sons to help when a repair job must be done. By including their sons, they are showing them what men do. By making the experience pleasant, they are teaching them to enjoy the activity.

*A man must learn to adopt certain attitudes toward work and authority.* Little boys realize early on that father goes to work. Although this is often true of mother too, especially over the past couple of decades, it is primarily upon father that sons model themselves when it comes to matters involving work. Father is the child's first authority figure: it is father who expects accomplishments and the achievement of goals. As the son ages, it is his father who typically issues directions and assigns household chores. In his position of authority, the father teaches the son about authority relationships and what is and is not tolerated in the context of such relationships.

## Relationships With Women

As a child, you had to be prepared for relationships with women. A man must learn how to treat and deal with women. By the manner in which father deals with mother, he teaches many things—among them what a man should expect in a relationship with a woman, the skills needed to negotiate conflicts with a woman, the degree of emotional expressiveness that's appropriate for both men and women in intimate relationships, and what behaviors are expected of a man in the context of such a relationship. As the son matures and is able to assimilate more information, father also imparts information (through direct instruction and modeling) about the importance of fidelity in a relationship with a woman, and how to assess a woman by weighing her loyalty and kindness and observing the manner in which she treats others.

Additional skills and attitudes can be identified. For example, Robert Bly observes that typical fathers impart a love of spontaneity, respect for risk-taking, liveliness, a desire to penetrate, a love of action, and a love of knowledge. Psychiatrist Kyle Pruett, who undertook a long-term study of children raised in families in which father was the primary caretaker, speaks of father's tendency to cultivate (in both boys and girls) such traits as persistence, curiosity, and an ability to take pleasure in high levels of external stimulation.

## Exercise
### Lessons Your Father Taught You

What did your father teach you about being a man? Below are several topics in which you likely received instruction from him. Jot down any others on a separate sheet of paper. In the column labeled *Comments*, you may want to make notes on how your father taught you this lesson and the circumstances under which you learned it.

| Lesson | Comments |
|---|---|
| The importance of being able to compete | _____ |
| How to compete fairly | _____ |
| How to formulate and pursue goals | _____ |
| The importance of persistence | _____ |
| The importance of discipline and self-control | _____ |
| Being able to make sacrifices | _____ |
| How to put up with failure and disappointment | _____ |
| How to participate in and enjoy typical male activities | _____ |
| How to do minor repairs | _____ |
| How to participate in running a household (including shopping, cooking, etc.) | _____ |
| How to work and satisfy the expectations of others | _____ |
| How to deal with authority figures | _____ |
| How to treat women | _____ |
| What to expect in a relationship with a woman | _____ |
| How to negotiate conflicts with a woman | _____ |

The degree of emotional
expressiveness appropriate
for men                                    _____

Expectations a man must
fulfill within an intimate
relationship                               _____

The importance of fidelity
in a relationship                          _____


# The Father and Self-Esteem

Your father's impact on your self-esteem may well be his most
profound influence. Before assessing this, it's important to understand what self-esteem is and see why it is important.

The phrase *self-esteem* refers to your unconscious and unspoken attitude, positive or negative, toward yourself. It is a
global self-estimate in the sense that it's not tied to any particular set of circumstances or any particular relationship; instead
it cuts across every situation and relationship in which you engage.

Self-esteem is made up both of self-confidence and a sense
of self-worth. The former is reflected in your belief that you are
capable. The latter is reflected in the belief that you are deserving of respect and regard. Self-confidence is a transitory thing:
at times you may feel a lack of it; but you don't necessarily suffer from low self-regard.

To face life realistically and effectively, everyone must
have good self-esteem. Without it, you'll shrink from challenges,
accept shoddy treatment from others, and believe yourself un-
deserving of success.

A person's self-esteem has its origins in childhood experience. It's during childhood that you begin realizing that you
have talents, intelligence, and self-discipline. It's also the time
when you fail a great deal as you struggle to master new skills

and acquire huge amounts of information. The support, encouragement, and reassurance you receive during this critical time profoundly shapes what you think and feel about yourself. If you carry into adulthood a healthy self-regard, you're able to accept your strengths and weaknesses. You have a realistic sense of your intelligence, diligence, and of the appropriateness of your behavior. Seeing yourself realistically, you like yourself. You feel okay.

Your father was uniquely positioned to influence your self-esteem, both directly and indirectly. As the family representative of the outside world, his approval and recognition counted a great deal. Further, his love felt more conditional, whereas mother's was likely to feel unconditional. In your eyes he was the repository of the world's expectations. Once again, his reactions to your efforts shaped your view of yourself.

Indirectly, your father's crucial place in the family gave his behavior tremendous importance. If he modeled confidence and discipline, if he expected success, if he worked with diligence to achieve goals, then you likely came to believe yourself capable of the same kind of behavior. On the other hand, if your father modeled undesirable traits—lack of confidence, pessimism, the avoidance of challenges, and lack of persistence, for example—then you may well have come to expect those same behaviors in yourself.

## Errors Even Conscientious Fathers Make

In responding to his son, the conscientious father can err in two possible directions: he can expect too much, or he can expect too little.

If father expects too much—if he is perfectionistic and unrelenting in his demands—several predictable adverse consequences follow. Here are the most important:

- Because the son is unsuccessful in earning father's praise and love, he comes to believe that he is incompetent, unlovable, and unworthy. He believes that he can't succeed. The plight of a former patient will serve to illustrate this. The son of a brilliant and demanding father, this young man had had a very difficult time establishing himself. He'd dropped out of college as a sophmore and had gone from one third-rate job to another. Testing revealed that he had above-average intelligence and was functioning far below his capacities. His background appears to have been a major factor. He explained simply, "I grew up hearing over and over that I just wasn't good enough. I guess eventually I believed it."

- The son avoids testing himself. He may not try at all when challenged, or he may give up prematurely when faced with a difficult task. "I can't do this," he'll say to himself, not for any objective reason but because of a profound inner sense that he is incompetent. Such men miss out on a great deal in their lives. They are dropouts, the quitters, the husbands who leave marriages prematurely, the workers who leave jobs when the going gets tough. I recall one man, a construction foreman, who was asked to take over the construction of a building. The project had gotten off to a bad start and had long been problematical. Although this foreman was relatively inexperienced, his positive attitude and ambition had influenced his superiors to put him to the test by putting him in charge of this difficult job. It was obvious after a few weeks that he needed more training in specific areas if he was going to see the construction project through. However, he was afraid to ask for training, despite the fact that the company he worked for was quite willing to invest money and time in its employees. Instead, he bolted, impulsively quitting his job.

- The son has real difficulties in authority-subordinate relationships. He may resent authority figures and view them as impossible to satisfy. Unaware of the fact that such reactions are holdovers from childhood, he views himself as unlucky, since he always seems to wind up working for people who are unrealistic in their demands and woefully slow to offer the praise and support he craves so desperately.

- The son undermines his own efforts to succeed. He may unconsciously forget key elements in a project of which he's in charge, sabotaging his success. He may fail to consult with the necessary superiors before making a crucial decision, ensuring that his otherwise good work fails for political reasons.

Now consider what happens in the opposite case, when father expects too little. If he praises indiscriminately and fails to uphold a standard, several predictable adverse consequences follow. Here are the most important:

- The son comes to expect acceptance, admiration, and love without having to earn them. Since he's never learned that it's necessary to work for recognition, he expects it to be provided by the world at large simply because he is who he is. He is invariably resentful and disillusioned later on.

- The son is unprepared to strive: to face and overcome obstacles, to work with diligence, commitment, and discipline to achieve his goals. Many a capable but untrained musician has failed to fulfill his talent because he got by on a good ear. He was enthusiastically praised for his innate talent that he never realized the ultimate importance of study and hard work.

- The son never learns to accept responsibility for his failures. Because of his inflated and unrealistic beliefs about himself, he is quick to blame others or "circumstances" when something he's in charge of goes wrong. He gets away with this once in a while; but his tendency to repeatedly resort to fault-finding eventually catches up with him. He never learns that it's he who must grow and change if he is to succeed. Thus, he limits his growth by failing to look objectively and realistically at his own part in his failures.

- The son is unable to distinguish between good and flawed work (and behavior) on his part. In his eyes, everything he does is praiseworthy. If others fail to recognize the high quality of his performance, the problem is theirs and not his. Such a man will often go from one job to another, and from one relationship to another. He fails to catch on to the fact that the disappointment of others is based on a realistic appraisal of the quality of what he does and his behavior in intimate relationships.

- The son may be intolerant of criticism and frustration. Because he believes that he is virtually beyond criticism, he is disinclined to listen—even to well-meaning and sincere people who are offering criticism for his own good. Similarly, when he is frustrated by circumstances or other people, he is likely to lose his temper or otherwise behave disagreeably. He's simply too used to having things go his way.

- The son may be quick to give up in the face of challenges. Ironically, this tendency is common both to men of whom too much has been expected and to men of whom too little has been expected. In the latter case, the tendency to give up prematurely stems from the man's unwillingness and inability to look at his own part in the difficulty he is encountering. Instead, he blames people, timing, circumstances—anything but himself.

## Unconscientious Fathers

Although overly conscientious fathers can have an adverse impact on their sons, far more sinister and destructive are the fathers who fail to perform their role adequately. They may be uninvolved, indifferent, or uncaring. Worse still, they may be abusive, addicted, or otherwise monstrous.

All the problems of sons discussed in the previous section of the chapter are dramatically heightened when the son has been fathered by an uncaring or abusive father. For example, whereas the conscientious father who expects too much creates a son who believes he cannot win love or acceptance, the abusive or uncaring father wounds a son far more deeply, creating a profound despair and sense of unworthiness. Similarly, a father who expects too little may create a son who fails to accept responsibility for his behavior; but the abusive or uncaring father fails altogether even to impart the notion of responsibility to his child. Such deep wounds may require intensive therapy. To change, the son of such a man must work hard to develop insight and change his thinking and behavior (see Chapter 9 for specific techniques). Without real effort, these men are likely to become the deviants, the sociopaths and criminals (white collar and otherwise) who drain society's resources and destroy all that's good in the world.

More will be said about inadequate fathering throughout this book.

# Exercise
## *Assessing Your Self-Esteem*

Below is a list of descriptive statements that address the matter of your self-esteem. Look at each statement and determine whether or not the statement is mostly true of you. It may be that not all the statements will be relevant to your particular situation—just consider the ones that are. If the statements in Parts 1 and 2 describe you well, chances are that your self-esteem is good. If the statements in Parts 3 and 4 are descriptive of you, chances are that your self-esteem is shaky.

## Part 1: Indications of Good Self-Esteem

- When faced with an obstacle that stands between me and something I want, I usually feel confident that I can overcome it.

- I've always expected to succeed in life and have long been certain that I possess the strength, drive, and determination to reach my goals.

- I have little difficulty establishing and maintaining satisfying relationships with superiors to whom I am accountable (bosses, managers, teachers, and so on).

- I have little difficulty establishing and maintaining satisfying relationships with subordinates who are accountable to me.

## Part 2: Positive Childhood Experiences

- When I was growing up, my father almost always conveyed a belief in me and my abilities. I knew that he believed in me, no matter how difficult things got between us.

- When I was growing up, my father showed his love for me directly and unmistakably.

- My father always seemed interested in things I did—my schooling, my hobbies, and so on. He expected a lot of me; but he was proud of my accomplishments and managed to make me feel good about myself, even when I screwed up.

## Part 3: Negative Childhood Experiences

- My father typically treated me with indifference, rarely taking the time to acknowledge my strengths or show his appreciation of my efforts.

- I recall my father being actively abusive (physically, psychologically, or both) toward me or other members of my family.

- When I look back on my childhood, I realize that my father was too uncritical of me and expected too little of me. Though I welcomed the chance to get away with things, I realize now that he often took the easy way out by not insisting that I do things properly; as a result, I never learned how.

- My father was a hypercritical person, always demanding and never satisfied with my efforts, no matter how hard I tried to live up to his standards.

## Part 4: Indications of Problems With Self-Esteem

- I have a hard time feeling good about myself when I know that others whose opinions matter are displeased with me or my work.

- I have a more difficult time tolerating criticism than most people. I don't like having my weaknesses pointed out by others. Because my sense of personal worth crumbles when I'm criticized, I typically look for ways to defend myself when I'm criticized, rather than keeping an open mind and trying to learn from what the critic is telling me.

- I am decidedly more uncomfortable than most people when I am put to the test and must demonstrate my ability or skill in a high-pressure situation.

- I have a more difficult time tolerating frustration than most people.

- To an unusual degree, I expect my superiors (bosses, teachers, or others who have authority over me) to be protective and supportive. I especially like being the apple of their eye, a sort of superstar who can do no wrong.

- In my view, love, acceptance, and success are things that other people will experience in their lives. Somehow, I don't expect to experience them in mine.

- More than most people, I seem to be subject to depression and feelings of loneliness.

- I've learned that I tend to work very inefficiently in my efforts to realize my goals.

- Being liked by others is very important to me. When I'm in a position of authority, I sometimes avoid exercising leadership and making decisions because I fear that what I say or do will be unpopular with my subordinates.

- In many of my close relationships I play a fairly dependent role, often inviting my partner to rescue or take care of me.

Although the preceding inventory isn't offered as a scientific measure of your self-esteem, it can help you gauge the extent to which your experiences with your father had a positive or negative effect on your sense of self-worth. Bear in mind that human dynamics are always complicated. Many of the statements in Part 1 may be true for you, even if most of the statements in Parts 3 and 4 are true for you as well. Our parents are usually not just one way with us, but an amalgam of often conflicting behaviors. How your self-esteem fared has to do with a variety of factors, including your successes and failures as a child and the strengths and weaknesses of your relationships with others.

# To Summarize

This chapter was intended to give you a sense of the range of your father's influence. You learned about his importance in helping you separate from your mother, and about his role in helping you establish a secure sense of identity as a male. You were introduced to some of the many skills that sons must learn if they are to function as males, and you saw your father's role as the transmitter of these crucial cultural expectations. Finally, you got some idea of how your father influenced your self-esteem. In the next chapter, you'll look at means by which fathers influence their sons.

# Recommended Reading

Bly, R. (1990) *Iron John: A Book About Men*. Reading, MA: Addison-Wesley.

Erikson, E. (1958) *Young Man Luther*. New York: W. W. Norton.

Hardy, M., and J. Hough (1991) *Against the Wall: Men's Reality in a Codependent Culture*. New York: Ballantine Books.

Levant, R., and J. Kelly. (1989) *Between Father and Child: How To Become the Kind of Father You Want To Be*. New York: Penguin Books.

Pruett, K. (1987) *The Nurturing Father: Journey Toward the Complete Man*. New York: Warner Books.

Tannen, D. (1990) *You Just Don't Understand*. New York: Ballantine Books.

Vogt, G. M., and S. T. Stirridge. (1991) *Like Son, Like Father: Healing the Father-Son Wound in Men's Lives*. New York: Plenum Press.

# 3

# How Fathers Shape
# Their Sons

In this chapter, you'll learn about the ways in which fathers mold their sons. As suggested in Chapter 1, there are socially and culturally imposed limitations on what men can say: they exert most of their influence not directly, by sharing their inner selves, but rather indirectly. The two vehicles upon which men rely most heavily are modeling—demonstrating through their own behavior how to think, feel, and act—and metaphor—conveying beliefs, attitudes, and skills by instructing their sons in sports and encouraging their participation in other stereotypical male activities.

# How Fathers Exert Influence Indirectly

In our culture, men are usually expected to play the role of economic provider. There is a culturally imposed cloak of silence that veils a father's inner life—his feelings, concerns, and needs—from the direct view of others, including his son.

Because a father cannot say many things directly, he communicates most of the time by what he does rather than verbally. He behaves a particular way in the hope that his son will understand the meaning of his behavior, and will learn by observing.

Here's the sort of thing I mean: a father typically shows his love for his son by doing small things that say a great deal. For example, he might teach his son to ride a bike, take him sailing, or insist that the family go camping a few times a year. In doing so, he is sharing with his boy his own love of the outdoors. While such general actions may seem to carry little emotional weight, his behavior may be as direct an expression of his love as he feels capable of making.

For their part, sons learn early not to expect from father the same kind of direct emotional communication they get from mom. They come to expect obtuse, indirect messages of caring and love from dad. Ironically, father isn't always equally indirect in communicating his anger or displeasure: he has our culture's permission to be quite direct in expressing these.

Father also provides indirect instruction in how to be a man by the way he behaves. For example, his way of doing a job or negotiating conflicts with his wife serves as a model for his son.

Sons learn important lessons about male behavior by observing father. They watch him, then begin to imitate him in their thinking, outlook, and behavior. Anthropologists have long recognized that imitation is a common tool by which important lessons are conveyed in every culture. Edward T. Hall calls learning by imitation *informal learning*. He distinguishes it from *formal learning*, which occurs when one's errors are corrected, and *technical learning*, the kind that occurs in the classroom.

Thus the son will learn the masculine way to respond to a wide range of experiences by watching his father's responses. By seeing how his father reacts to failure or disappointment, the son learns the way a man is supposed to respond. By watching him deal with frustration, the son learns how he should do so, too. By seeing the way his father solves problems, the son learns a man's approach to problem-solving.

The son also learns how to behave toward women by observing how his father treats his mother and other women. Dad's treatment of a daughter, for example, is likely to be more affectionate and gentle than his treatment of his son. As a result of observing this, the son gets the message that women are supposed to be handled gently and affectionately. By contrast, the implied message comes across that men are not supposed to be fussed over or treated with tenderness—at least not by other men.

## Exercise
### *Assessing the Influence of Your Own Father's Behavior*

Here's another version of the checklist in Chapter 2 of lessons your father taught you. As you think about the various lessons you learned, ask yourself: Did I learn this by watching the way he behaved? Did I ever set out to imitate him—for example, in the way I dealt with a problem or another person? Bear in mind that your father's behavior may have given you a negative message. If he screamed at your mother every time the household was short of money, he gave you the implicit message that failure and frustration should be dealt with by blaming someone else. Note both the negative and positive messages conveyed by your father's behavior.

| **Lesson** | **How I Was Influenced by My Father's Behavior** |
|---|---|
| The importance of being able to compete | _____ |
| How to compete fairly | _____ |
| How to formulate and pusue goals | _____ |
| The importance of persistence | _____ |
| The importance of discipline and self-control | _____ |
| Being able to make sacrifices | _____ |
| How to put up with failure and disappointment | _____ |
| How to participate in and enjoy typical male activities | _____ |
| How to do minor repairs | _____ |
| How to participate in running a household | _____ |
| How to work and satisfy the expectations of others | _____ |
| How to deal with authority figures | _____ |
| How to treat women | _____ |
| What to expect in a relationship with a woman | _____ |
| How to negotiate conflicts with a woman | _____ |
| The degree of emotional expressiveness appropriate for men | _____ |

Expectations a man must
fulfill within an intimate
relationship
_____

The importance of fidelity in
a relationship
_____

## How Fathers Exert Influence
## Through Modeling

Men convey three main types of information to their sons.

### Specific Attitudes, Skills, and Behaviors
### Required for Day-to-Day Living

Fathers model ways of coping as a man. Depending on their own temperaments, and the emotional adjustments they've made, they demonstrate the coping strategies they've chosen— whether negative or positive. Some fathers fail to prepare their sons for life because they themselves are ill-prepared to manage. Others display highly refined coping skills.

Let's suppose that a man is doing a household repair job. In the middle of it, he realizes that he needs a tool he doesn't own. Suppose further that a neighbor owns the precise tool he wants. He discusses the matter briefly with his wife and decides to ask their neighbor if he can borrow the tool. The way he prepares for the conversation with his neighbor, the words he uses when he speaks, his manner in making the request and acknowledging the assistance—all these serve to show the son how a man gets his needs met. The father's behavior may model how to receive a kindness graciously, without vilifying others or creating resentment; or he may inadvertently teach his son that it's awkward and unpleasant for a man to be indebted to someone else for a favor.

Here's another example. A husband and wife are planning to repaint their bedroom. They disagree over the color. Rather than argue, however, the husband yields to his wife's preference. By acquiescing, the man is demonstrating that his wife's happiness can sometimes take precedence over his own. On other occasions, he demonstrates that it's appropriate at times to assert his preference. Perhaps his wife has given permission to their son to take hang-gliding lessons. The father knows about the dangers of hang-gliding, and puts his foot down, feeling that the sport is unsafe and inappropriate for their 15-year-old. When he's 18, he can decide to learn hang-gliding if he still wants to.

Finally, a father models how to direct and to accept direction by how he shares leadership in the family. For example, he may assume leadership responsibilities on matters of family finances, while accepting his wife's leadership when it comes to maintaining cordial relationships with the extended family.

## How To Respond to Events

As a son watches his father respond to specific events, the youngster learns how men behave toward others. He also learns what he should expect of himself. The issue of how to acknowledge and deal with pain will illustrate clearly what I mean.

Does a father acknowledge his own pain? Suppose his daughter fails to include him in an important confidence she's made to her mother—such as that she's decided to change her major at college. It's clear that he feels hurt, but does he show any vulnerability? Or does he react by getting angry or ignoring his daughter's behavior? Repeated experiences of this sort model "appropriate" male behavior under similar circumstances.

How does the father react when others are in pain? In the normal course of events, a father and son will witness many painful incidents together. Suppose the boy's little sister falls and scrapes her knee. She cries out in pain, and father is solicitous and tender toward her. A little brother does the same and father is somewhat less solicitous. Perhaps he even exchanges glances with his older son, suggesting silently that the child's younger brother is a sissy for having made such a fuss over a scraped knee. The lesson is unmistakable: women have permission to cry aloud when in pain; men don't.

Perhaps the son himself is injured in the course of playing softball with his father. The son misses a catch and the ball strikes him in the face. On the verge of tears, he looks to his father, hoping for comfort. Quite deliberately, but without malice, the father chooses to ignore his son's hurt. Instead, he urges the son on to get the ball, yelling that the runner will score if the son doesn't throw to home plate. By ignoring the boy's pain, the father is clearly suggesting that it's unimportant within the context of competing effectively among other men.

In addition to modeling the kinds of specific lessons just discussed, fathers also model *life scripts*—patterns of behavior and thinking that are played out over a lifetime.

## *Modeling Life Scripts*

A life script sets out the broad parameters for a man's existence: it is a set of directions for playing out one's part in life. For the purposes of this book, I've identified ten male life scripts, among them the long-suffering father and the angry father. Although one of these ten scripts usually predominates in a man, almost everyone tailors the script to the particular circumstances of his life and moves from script to script at various times.

Each of the ten scripts is presented by means of a brief vignette. At the end of each description, I've pointed out the feelings most frequently evoked by the type of man characterized, and summarized what each one teaches his son about what it means to be a man. Finally, there's a brief first-hand account by someone who was raised by the type of father described.

As you read the descriptions that follow, try to determine which of them typifies your own father. Think, too, about whether your father revised his script, or adopted new ones, during the course of his life. I'd like you also to consider the extent to which your view of manhood was shaped by your father's life script.

### The Saintly, Long-Suffering Father

This man is a hard worker who has a tendency to take care of everyone but himself. He experiences little joy in life. Unfailingly industrious, patient, and tolerant, he expects little satisfaction from other people or from life in general. He makes few demands on family members, but takes on his own shoulders almost the entire responsibility for satisfying the family's demands. He is a quiet, strong, and unappreciated man who receives very little but gives a great deal. He evokes feelings of pity and guilt. He teaches the lesson that manhood is a dreadful obligation.

New York's leading Democrat, Mario Cuomo, was fathered by such a man. Commenting on whether his father was an affectionate man, Cuomo observed in a *New Yorker* profile: "I think of him as being very affectionate, but I don't remember him putting his arm around me. You always had the sense that he had great feeling for you. You saw him providing for you, at enormous pain to himself. You saw him doing nothing for himself— never bought himself anything, never enjoyed himself.... So the overwhelming impression we got was that this man was offering us his life: he didn't have to put his arm around you."

### The Heroic Father

This man is extraordinarily courageous. Physically imposing, he does things other men are afraid to do. He may be a fireman, a policeman, a construction worker, or someone else involved in a physically demanding job. As a result of his gruff exterior, people fear and respect him, but they're also intimidated by him. Most of his friendships are superficial and fleeting. Rather than liking him, people see him as tough and awe-inspiring: he's most likely to evoke a fearful respect in others. His lesson about manhood is that it is bound up with strength and power; but, ultimately, a man is alone.

One man I interviewed was fathered by such a man. After running away from home at 14 to join the circus, this man's father left his native Germany and traveled the world. Over the years he had been a sailor, a mercenary, and an actor. He had led safaris in Africa and worked at a variety of dangerous jobs— at one time he was a lumberjack in the Pacific Northwest. His son observed: "We have a picture of him when he came out of the lumber camps. He weighed 250 pounds, and you could see there wasn't an ounce of fat on him. He was big! And he was well-known all throughout our town for his strength." Several times during the interview, this man referred proudly to the fact that people were afraid of his father. The son himself was in awe of his father's almost superhuman strength and his enormous presence.

### The Super-Achieving, Workaholic Father

This man is resoundingly successful, and has all the material trappings to prove it. He may be a high-ranking executive or government official who travels the world confidently, engaged in important business. He is effective and bold and widely respected. He has few close friends, however, since most of his waking hours are spent working, preparing for work, or winding down from work. Virtually all of his relationships outside the family are with people who want to use his power and prestige to their own advantage, or who simply enjoy being in the company of movers and shakers. Within his family, a man like this remains a stranger to his wife and children. He is often physically absent and almost always emotionally withdrawn. His lesson about manhood is that it is bound up with achievement: work is the only real satisfaction for a man, although success isolates him from others.

One man described his super-successful father this way: "He was always wrapped up in his work. He lived it and breathed it! It was his only excitement. Sometimes he'd be away for weeks at a time. And when he was home, it wasn't like things were normal, even then. I remember he'd bring his work home, and there were just reams and reams of paper. He was just going over it, over and over. Sometimes I look back on it and I wonder what he was trying to escape from."

### The Self-Contained Father

This man appears to be untouched by pain or injury. He never seems to be vulnerable, weak, or needy: his entire life reflects a stubborn inner strength. Because he is uncomplaining and self-sufficient, he has trouble with the give-and-take of relationships: he's uncomfortable being at the receiving end. As a result, he tends to be emotionally isolated, even though a great many people may admire him. If he were to become seriously ill, he would conceal it from his family and colleagues for as long as possible. (In extreme cases, he might even contrive elaborate explanations to mask symptoms or account for absences from work.) He evokes feelings of reverence. He teaches that a real man is self-sufficient and tough, and that he remains aloof and distant, even from the people closest to him.

One of the men I interviewed recalled that his physician father waged a long and ultimately losing battle with heart disease, dying in his early fifties. But he kept the gravity of his illness to himself, lying outright to his patients, and minimizing the seriousness of his condition to his family. "Several times my father checked himself into the hospital for days at a time," the son recalled. "He used to tell his patients he was going on vacation. My mother went along with his downplaying how sick he was. We all just accepted his reassurances."

### The Secretly Vulnerable Father

To the outside world, this man appears to be strong, competent, pleased with his life, and even invulnerable. Within the immediate family, however, he is very sad and decidedly vulnerable. He may be victimized by his wife, his parents, or his employer. He doesn't talk to anyone about his feelings, and no one is allowed to confront or disturb him by talking about his distress. The open secret of his wounded, vulnerable nature cannot be explicitly discussed. The feelings he evokes within his family are pity and sadness. The message he teaches about manhood is that men must learn to present to the world a pretense of strength in order to mask their vulnerability.

"My father looked and seemed a lot more intact than he was," said one man I spoke with. "So far as anybody could tell, he was a strong, capable man. But at home, it was another story. He was weak, indecisive. He couldn't deal with my mother, who was angry with him for a lot of things; she used to run him down in front of me and my brothers. He was a really amazingly ineffectual man. He never had the guts to stand up to her. And he didn't respect himself for it. Eventually, we all lost respect for him."

### The Depressed Father

This man lives a joyless life, struggling daily with a depression that is always threatening to overwhelm him. He manages to hold a job and go through the motions of living, but he dislikes almost everything about his life: his wife, his children, his work. He wishes he were somebody else, living someplace else, with other people. He lives continually with a great sadness, disappointment, and frustration. Despite occasional outward successes, he sees himself and his life as a failure. He does not talk about this with anyone, but often cannot hide his feelings. In the usual course of events, he manages to hold on emotionally and escape his pain by isolating himself from the family and becoming absorbed in endless TV watching, in sleeping, and other escapist activities. He may undergo periodic emotional collapses, occasionally drinking, abusing drugs, or womanizing to escape his dreadful feelings of failure. He evokes feelings of pity and guilt. The lesson his son learns is that men must suffer through the unhappiness and disappointment of life.

One man told me, "I just knew my father had absolutely no joy in his life. He'd come home from work—he hated his job and the people he worked with, but he had very specialized skills, so there weren't many places he could work—and sit in his chair. He'd be quiet, like we weren't there at all. Just stare into space. I'd go up and ask him a question, 'Hey, Dad, want to do this, that, and the other thing?' He'd just sit there and wouldn't answer."

### The Angry Father

This man is perfectionistic and harshly judgmental. He makes impossible demands on his wife and children and is furious when they don't measure up. Rarely soft or tender, he is almost always either enraged or on the verge of losing his temper. When family members are around him, they "walk on eggshells," afraid they'll set him off. He is rarely relaxed, but a good deal of the family's energy goes toward keeping things smooth so he won't get upset. He seldom leaves family members with the feeling that they've satisfied him. A bully by nature, he evokes feelings of terror and resentment. His lesson is that life is a lousy business where the strong bully the weak and psychological or physical violence is the way men survive.

One young man told about his father, who modeled this script: "He always cut me down. Whenever I did something, it was never right. If we were doing a project and I finished my part, he'd say, 'You could've done it a lot quicker.' And he was explosive." One day at dinner, as an older teen, the man made a snide remark about his father. "I remember he got up out of his chair and swung at me across the table. I grabbed his hand. I guess he saw the steel in my eyes. He sat back down."

### The Chemically Addicted Father

This man relies on alcohol or drugs to make it through his day-to-day life. Family members learn not to acknowledge his addiction, and they conscientiously avoid addressing the emotional and family problems bound up with it. To the outside world, this man may appear to be normal. Family members cover for him, making excuses (for example, to his employer) and otherwise concealing the truth from outsiders. When he is drunk or high, he may be morose, or explosive, or abusive. He evokes mixed feelings of rage, pity, and deep resentment. The lesson he teaches about manhood is that it is an ugly masquerade, a pretense of competence.

One fireman, well-know in his department for his daring and courage, spoke to me at great length about his alcoholic father. "I remember the night he was going to kill us all, with a knife. He came home drunk, and I mean drunk. Not just feeling good. He was gone! In another world, okay? My mother had to wrestle the knife away from him. And she was able to do it because she was pretty strong herself, and because he was so drunk. But there's no doubt in my mind, and in hers, that he would've killed us all. And you would've read about it in the paper the next day if she wasn't there."

### The Sweet, Nice Guy

This man is gentle to a fault and not at all typically masculine in his outlook on life. Too eager to please others, he is uncomfortable wielding authority and over concerned about hurting other people's feelings. Though he can't be called feminine, he is characterized by a sort of pseudo-femininity that shows itself in an exaggerated delicacy and horror of confrontation. It's difficult for a son to rebel or test himself against this kind of father, because the man fails to provide a solid ground against which a son can differentiate himself. Such men are tentative and equivocal in their opinions. They often sulk when they do not get what they want, evoking mixed feelings of pity and contempt. They teach that to be a man in the conventional sense of the term is somehow shameful.

Said one man, "My father was a lousy excuse for a man. One time when I was in high school, I was suspended for supposedly throwing candy around in the school library—I guess I was in the tenth grade. He refused to go to bat for me, even though I really hadn't thrown the candy! I was a good student; I just happened to be in the library when these guys started goofing off. I went home really upset and asked mom and dad to go up to school about it. Dad thought it over and decided it wasn't worth making a fuss over. Maybe to him it wasn't—but I was innocent! That really bothered me! He was like that in other things, too. He was a frightened man. As I got older, it became clearer and clearer that he relied on my mother to deal with people and situations he was too scared to handle."

### The Competent, Nurturing Father

All of the scripts discussed so far have been negative. But, of course, many fathers are well-balanced, competent, and nurturing. Such men model a script that is characterized by reliability, consistency, appropriate use of male strength, and the ability to be tender. They are by no means unmasculine. They can nurture, be tuned in to the emotional currents in the family, and be sensitive to the needs of wife and children. Sons fathered by such men recall them as being solid and supportive. These competent, well-balanced fathers have grown beyond the cultural stereotype of masculinity. They are simultaneously strong and soft, tough and tender, authoritative and caring, demanding and compassionate. The lesson they teach is that manhood is a way of dealing with self and others which is rooted in love, supported by strength, and bounded by self-respect.

One man described his father, who had been born into poverty. He grew up on the streets of New York in the 20s and 30s—so he had learned to be tough. "But there was a tender side to him. He really loved my mother and you knew it. He's the one who paid for my college and graduate school, even though it wasn't easy; and he was always supportive, unlike many of the men he'd grown up with: most of their kids never even had the chance to go to college. The few who did dropped out—partly, I think, because their fathers never really approved.

"My father was the kind of man who could be sensitive, yet he was a man's man. He loved to cook, and he'd make wonderful meals! It was he who helped me feel comfortable in the kitchen. Yet there was no mistaking that he wanted me and my brothers to better ourselves. He expected a lot of us, and, except for one brother, we all lived up to his expectations. Even at his toughest, he was the kind of man who was easy to talk to. You respected him because he was emotionally *there*, and very sure of himself."

# How Fathers Exert Influence Through Metaphor

The second major tool by which fathers shape sons is metaphor. Many of the activities fathers share with sons or teach them to participate in are metaphors—vehicles by which a man symbolically imparts lessons needed to survive and prosper in life. These lessons usually fall into two broad categories: sports and accepted "masculine" activities.

## Sports

It's no accident that, for many fathers and sons, sports serve as a bridge between generations. Fathers typically place a great deal of emphasis on teaching sons how to play sports, and take great pride in their sons' accomplishments.

For their part, sons willingly go along with this business of learning to play sports, often for reasons they cannot adequately articulate. To them, learning sports is most often a chance to spend time with dad.

One father I interviewed spent a great deal of time talking about how much he and his son enjoy golfing together. He told me about the pride he takes in seeing his son play. "I love to watch him!" he observed, adding quickly that when his son gets upset at having hit a bad shot, the father counsels him: "I say to him, 'What are you doing? The first rule is you gotta forget the last shot and think about the next one! Otherwise you're going to take a 15 on this hole!'" His words are significant. Golf for him was a way of teaching his son about the mental discipline needed to erase memories of failure and start fresh in order to succeed.

Sports are metaphorical on several levels. As has often been observed, all sports are forms of ritual combat. They teach competitiveness, persistence, and fortitude—how to compete, how to win, and how to lose. Many sports teach boys how to share responsibility, to be a "team player": what it means to be fair and, as more experienced team members serve as models, how to respond when treated unfairly. Boys learn from participating in sports that skill-building is a slow, laborious process—that it's important to be patient and take a long view of things.

One man I spoke with fondly recalled the pleasure he took in playing throughout his teens in local men's doubles tennis tournaments with his father. As the years passed, the two became a powerful team, and about half the time made it into the final rounds of the tournaments they played in. (He recalled proudly that they earned eight trophies, one of which was a first-place cup.) This experience was a remarkably rich one, with father modeling the many skills and attitudes required to persist and succeed under pressure. The two also took doubles lessons together, and learned to cooperate in developing a game plan and implementing their strategy.

Another man remembered that, from the time he was a very young boy, his father went out of his way to spend time with him. He told me about the camping trips they took together and the Saturdays they'd spend fly-fishing. But his fondest memory, and his biggest thrill, occurred when he was a young teen. His dad would take him for excursions in the family van on backroads, and actually let him drive. These experiences were not only pleasurable in themselves, but they also created bonds between father and son, and conveyed the heady lesson that laws can be bent by responsible men in the course of teaching their sons the skills required for living.

## Accepted Masculine Activities

Doing fix-it jobs around the house, repairing and maintaining an auto, building things with wood, and related "man's work" are similar to sports in that they provide metaphorical lessons about life.

For example, auto maintenance and repair work teaches the value of careful observation and patience. It is also a way of teaching problem-solving skills. Many a father and son have spent a summer's day "tuning up the old Chevy" while the son was learning about life in the process.

Doing simple home repair jobs teaches many similar lessons, among them the value of systematic plans, organization, and self-discipline. For example, one man I interviewed was only nine years old when his father died. Though he had few memories of him, his clearest recollections were of projects he and his father had done around the house. He remembered repairing a doorbell and building a worktable in the basement. The man-to-man feeling of companionship had given these activities an almost magical quality, which was heightened when his father died. The man proudly noted that he is quite handy around the house even now, and that he takes great pleasure in maintaining his home. His experience captures the importance of such activities both in teaching skills and building connections between father and son.

## To Summarize

In this chapter you've learned why fathers so often rely on indirect influence in shaping and molding their sons. Prevented by culture from revealing much of their inner selves to their sons, men prepare their sons for life largely through modeling and metaphor. They show their sons how to think, feel, and behave as a man—and how to succeed as a man—by demonstrating appropriate male behaviors. They rely on sports and accepted masculine activities to teach important lessons metaphorically.

## Recommended Reading

Hall, E. T. (1959) *The Silent Language*. Greenwhich, CT: Fawcett Publications.

Osherson, S. (1986) *Finding Our Fathers: How a Man's Life Is Shaped by His Relationship With His Father.* New York: Fawcett-Columbine.

Steiner, C. (1974) *Scripts People Live.* New York: Grove Press.

# 4

# How Fathers Fail
# Their Sons

Effective fathering is essential to the son's establishing a secure male identity. When fathering is ineffective, either because it is inadequate or overbearing, the son has greater difficulty establishing that identity in a positive way.

In this chapter you'll learn more about why fathers play such a key role in helping their sons come to think of themselves as men. You'll also learn to recognize some of the differences between effective and ineffective fathering. Finally, you'll become familiar with four predictable ways in which sons suffer when the fathering they receive is ineffective.

# The Importance of Father

A boy's primary identification is with his mother. His masculine identity comes later, as a result of a process psychologists call *disidentification*, by which a boy distinguishes himself from mother and begins establishing a male identity. The complex process of disidentification is necessary in the life of the son, but not that of the daughter. Girls have confirmation of their identity as females when they start their periods. By contrast, the onset of puberty for boys is somewhat more ambiguous: a son must be "made" into a man. He must break his primary identification with mother and begin identifying with his father instead.

This need to make boys into men accounts for the male initiation ceremonies that are found in every preindustrial culture on earth. Although these ceremonies vary a great deal, they all have elements in common. According to mythologist Joseph Campbell, author of *The Hero With a Thousand Faces*, and scholar Mircea Eliade, a professor of religious history who authored *Rites and Symbols of Initiation*, all such ceremonies share the following qualities:

- The boy, usually near the onset of puberty, is forcibly removed from his mother, often under frightening and dramatic circumstances. For example, the men in the village disguise themselves and launch a terrifying raid on the mother's abode; they "kidnap" the child, carrying him away over his mother's protests.

- The boy is taken to an unfamiliar place for days or weeks and subjected to experiences that transform him. These can include fasting, burning, and prolonged exposure to the elements. This hazing symbolizes the end of childhood for the boy and sets him apart from his mother and the "feminine" world that he has come to know so well. He may also sit at the feet of elders who instill tribal teachings, sometimes in the form of myths and stories.

- Once initiated, the boy is given symbols of his new identity. He may be renamed and given a weapon or some other token of manhood. With his new status, he gains the right to behave as a man, assuming some of the responsibilities of the men in the tribe.

Since our society lacks group rites of initiation by which a boy is confirmed into manhood, responsibility falls primarily on the father to help make his son into a man. In psychological terms, the father must help the youngster disidentify with the mother and establish a primary identification with the father instead. This is a critically important responsibility; and yet it is not one that every father fulfills admirably.

Sons who are adequately fathered ultimately identify with the male image represented by their father and unselfconsciously come to think of themselves as male. They are comfortable being male and affirm their masculinity. Those who are fathered poorly or who are fatherless may lack a well-defined male image with which to identify. (I say "may" because fatherless and inadequately fathered boys are often remarkably creative in finding surrogate father figures to whom they become very attached and who serve the important purpose of providing a male image.) Men who are fatherless or who have been inadequately fathered may feel uncomfortable accepting their maleness and may not affirm their masculinity. I don't mean to imply by this that male homosexuality is in any sense caused by inadequate fathering. In fact, in relationships between gay men, one typically assumes the male role and behaves in ways that are unmistakably consistent with what our culture thinks of as being male.

Below is a list of traits and behaviors that are characteristic of ineffective fathers. The list is the product of my research and interviews I conducted for this book. In the middle column are relevant statements the son of such a father might formulate if he were asked to describe his father's presence during his childhood and adolescence. Each trait/statement combination points up one of the ways in which a father can fail his son. Consider each one, think back on your childhood and adolescence, and determine to what degree the statement describes your own father. In the righthand column, write *Never*, *Sometimes*, or *Always*, depending on the degree to which each statement matches your own father's behavior or attitudes.

| *Traits of Ineffective Fathers* | | |
|---|---|---|
| **Trait or Behavior** | **Son's Descriptive Statement** | **True of Your Own Father** *(Almost Never, Sometimes, Almost Always)* |
| Father was absent. | There were many times when I would've wanted to ask my father for help or advice, but he just wasn't there. | |
| Father was emotionally unavailable. | Although my father was physically present, he was most often preoccupied with matters that did not include me (his job, for example). | |
| Father was unattuned to the child's emotional needs. | On a number of important occasions, my father forgot promises he made me, and/or important events in my life (for example, school plays and music recitals). | |
| Father abused alcohol or drugs. | It was not unusual for me to see my father drunk or high on drugs. | |

| Traits of Ineffective Fathers | | |
|---|---|---|
| **Trait or Behavior** | **Son's Descriptive Statement** | **True of Your Own Father** (*Almost Never, Sometimes, Almost Always*) |
| Father was weak and ineffectual. | My father rarely stood up to my mother when important family issues came up. He was quick to give in if that would avoid a confrontation or argument. | |
| | My father was quite depressed much of the time. He seemed to be a defeated man, unable to stand up to the challenges posed by life. | |
| Father played an insignificant role in the day-to-day life of the child. | The parent who was mostly responsible for my upbringing was my mother. My father was present, but a peripheral figure. | |
| | When I had a problem or worry, I usually talked about it with my mother or someone else other than my father. | |
| | Around the time I reached puberty, I wished I could talk to my father about sex, but I couldn't. | |

| Traits of Ineffective Fathers | | |
|---|---|---|
| **Trait or Behavior** | **Son's Descriptive Statement** | **True of Your Own Father** (*Almost Never, Sometimes, Almost Always*) |
| Father was excessively demanding. | My father expected a great deal of me and seemed to be unrealistic about my capabilities. | |
| | I felt I was a disappointment to my father. | |
| Father was excessively judgmental. | My father tended to watch me very closely, monitoring and commenting critically on such things as my behavior and preferences, the friends I had, and my ways of passing time. | |
| | My father was quick to tell me what I *should* do, what I *should* want, and who I *should* be friends with. | |
| | My father typically made decisions for me. I often felt he took away my power—my right to live my life according to my own judgments and preferences. | |

| Traits of Ineffective Fathers | | |
| --- | --- | --- |
| **Trait or Behavior** | **Son's Descriptive Statement** | **True of Your Own Father** (*Almost Never, Sometimes, Almost Always*) |
| Father was physically threaltening or abusive. | I remember at least one occasion when my father threatened violence against me or some other family member. | |
| | My father used to beat my mother or other members of the family. | |
| | I remember at least one occasion when my father threatened suicide if things at home didn't go his way. | |
| Father was psychologically abusive. | My father belittled and demeaned my mother, me, or other members of the family. | |
| | My father manipulated family members psychologically, playing on guilt, shame, and other emotions. | |
| Father was extremely self-involved. | My father's top priority was himself. When he had free time or extra cash, he indulged himself, often at the expense of his family. | |

| Traits of Ineffective Fathers | | |
|---|---|---|
| **Trait or Behavior** | **Son's Descriptive Statement** | **True of Your Own Father** (*Almost Never, Sometimes, Almost Always*) |
| | I often had the feeling my father cared more about himself than about me or the rest of the family. | |
| Father was uninvolved with the family and uninterested in his children. | If my father was left to babysit for me or my siblings, he was quick to arrange for us to go off and play at a friend's house or get involved in something that didn't include him. He obviously had more interesting things to do than spend time with his kids. | |
| | My father was pretty unaware of the things I did or cared about. | |
| Father abandoned mother emotionally | My mother was lonely and unhappy. She looked to me for the emotional support my father didn't give her. | |

By adding and subtracting a few words, it's possible to convert the list into a description of the behaviors and characteristics of an effective father:

- He is physically present.

- He is emotionally available.

- He is in touch with his child's emotional needs.

- He does not abuse alcohol or drugs.

- He is strong and effective.

- He plays a significant role in the day-to-day life of his child.

- He is demanding, but realistically so within the context of his son's capabilities.

- He is mostly nonjudgmental.

- He is not physically threatening or abusive.

- He is not psychologically abusive.

- He is concerned and involved with his son and the family.

- He is interested in his son.

- He is an emotionally present companion to his wife.

In the next part of the chapter, you'll learn more specific details about the ways in which fathers fail their sons.

# Ineffective Fathering

In the course of discussing the behavior of ineffective fathers and its impact on their sons, I will draw on the firsthand accounts of men I interviewed in preparing to write this book.

There are two main types of ineffective fathering: inadequate and overbearing. Each type has several variations.

## Inadequate Fathering

By inadequate fathering I mean fathering that may provide for the physical welfare of the son, but nevertheless fails to meet his emotional, spiritual, and social-psychological needs. There are five variations on this inadequacy. All result in the son's lacking a strong, reliable male figure upon which to model his own behavior as a man.

### The Physically Absent Father

The physically absent father is not part of the child's normal, day-to-day life. He is not there to answer the youngster's questions, to listen when he is upset, to take over when an overtired mother needs relief.

How widespread is the problem of the physically absent father? According to Canadian psychoanalyst Guy Corneau, one in five children in the United States lives in a home with no father present. In Canada, one in seven children lives in such a home. Other writers present equally grim statistics. Sam Keen, former consulting editor of *Psychology Today*, has observed that 60 percent of children born in 1987 will not be living with or supported by their biological father when they reach adolescence. He further notes that nearly half of today's children are raised in single-parent families. (Corneau has reported that 89 percent of single-parent families in the United States are headed by women.) Psychiatrist Kyle Pruett reports that in 1985, 90 percent of American children of divorced families were in the custody of their mothers.

*Fathers who have abandoned their sons.* Some fathers are physically absent because they have abandoned their families altogether. One man I interviewed had attended boarding school from the age of seven because his father had abandoned the family. His mother received virtually no money from him; she had to work to make ends meet. Since she had no relatives nearby and could make no childcare arrangements (this was the early '40s), her only option was to send her son off to a boarding school. Doing so, she reasoned, would have one additional advantage: a boarding school would provide her son with males with whom he would be in regular contact and upon whom he could model himself. In the 40 years since his father had abandoned his family, the man I interviewed had never so much as received a letter from him. Asked what he would like to say to his father if the opportunity presented itself, he responded:

> I'd really grill him on his background, and what was going on in his mind, and why he left. He'd say my mother didn't want him, but I'd still want to know, why did he leave me? I'm sure my mother would never deny him access to me: to see me, to write to me, to talk to me, as I got older to take me out or whatever. I mean, he could've still been a father. So I would ask him, where was he all those years? What was he doing? I can't conceive of any possible excuse that he could have for not wanting to see me!

Of the void left in his father's absence, the man said simply:

> I guess you always have a father. With some people maybe the father gets killed off early or whatever. And there's a missing part of your life that's never there. That part of my life has always been missing. It will always be missing. You just learn to adapt.

*Fathers who are absent due to separation and divorce.* Other fathers are not part of the son's day-to-day life due to separation and divorce. Some maintain contact with their sons through conventional visitation, even though such contacts tend to be contrived and superficial. Many more, over time, drop out of the son's life altogether. One son described the situation this way:

> I'm resentful that I didn't grow up with a father. Little by little he became less and less involved and interested in our lives. I mean, he didn't take an interest when we were doing anything. He just [making the sound of a balloon losing air] faded right out!

Still, I'd like to see him. I'd like to ask him
why: why he never called us, why he never spent
time with us, why he wasn't interested in what we
were doing, why he never supported us, why he
did the things he did. I mean, if he was angry with
my mother, fine. That was something he had to
deal with. But why didn't he take any interest in
us? I mean, we were his children! You just take off
and not care?

## The Neglectful Father

The neglectful father is formally present in the child's life.
He hasn't left the family. Nevertheless, he is indifferent, uncaring, and uninvolved. He places little or no importance on raising
his son. Neglectful fathers are usually self-absorbed—not in activities from which the family may benefit, but in their hobbies,
their friends, and their life apart from the family.

Here is what one son had to say about his father:

My dad was a very social guy. He had all
kinds of interests and lots of friends. To him, my
mother and I were an afterthought. He was always
going someplace, involved with some project. He'd
visit friends. Every fall he'd spend weekend after
weekend hunting. When it came to schoolwork, my
mother was the one who helped me. If she had to
go out and he was left to take care of me, he'd
either get a babysitter and go on his way, or he'd
drag me wherever he was going and ignore me.

## The Emotionally Unavailable Father

Unlike the neglectful father, the emotionally unavailable
father is conscientious. He really tries to fulfill his role as father.
For a variety of reasons, though, he doesn't succeed. His priorities became distorted, and he overemphasizes his job or his own
emotional or physical wounds at the expense of his relationship

with his family. I'll focus on the workaholic father and the father whose physical illness or disabilities preoccupy him.

*Workaholic fathers.* A victim of gender stereotyping, the workaholic father defines his responsibility to his family very narrowly: his job is to protect and provide. In the end, he is unavailable and emotionally disconnected from his son.

One man told this story: His impoverished parents had emigrated from Europe in the early '30s. Within four years after arriving in the United States, they'd had three children. Shortly after the third child was born, the father opened a business. Almost all his time was spent "down at the shop." Over the next several years, he achieved remarkable financial success. But father and son had virtually no relationship at all. The material things provided by the father were a poor substitute for a normal family life.

> When I look back to when I was a child, I remember all my friends did a lot of things with their fathers. They were in Cub Scouts. Their fathers took them on trips. They went sailing. They horsed around together. We didn't really have that. The only thing I can remember doing with my father was once in a while we'd go swimming down at the country club. Basically, he'd give me things. He bought me a little sailboat. The two of us never went sailing, though. I got in trouble when I was a kid, and I think it might have been different if my family life had been stronger, you know? If the feelings had been expressed and there'd just been more between us.

Another man told a similar story. His father was immensely successful. Mechanically inclined, he made his fortune after the Second World War, reconditioning government surplus engines that he bought for pennies and resold for hundreds of dollars.

This son, like the one just quoted, comments on the father's tendency to substitute things for a relationship with his son. One example stood out in my interviewee's mind:

> For those days, he spent a great deal of money on some sort of [toy] helicopter. It was very disappointing. I mean, first of all, it wasn't me. It wasn't me at all! I was either too old for it or just not interested in those kinds of things. But he was interested in mechanical things. It was something that interested him. And the helicopter didn't work very well. You were supposed to pull the string and make the thing go around. It was supposed to fly. Well, it didn't. It just didn't do what it said on the box. And I was trying to give him what I felt he wanted, and, of course, he was disappointed. And it was just bad all the way around. It finally just petered out. I mean the helicopter didn't work. We tried a few times, and he went off to do something and I went off to do something.

A comment made by this son later in the interview sums things up better than I could:

> Our relationship was never as close or as satisfying as I would've wanted. We were very different men by the time he died. We had very little in common. We would've passed each other on the street without a second notice if we'd not been related by blood. What you get back to is I don't really know how he felt about things....

*Disabled fathers.* Sometimes tragedy places a barrier between father and son. Even the most conscientious father cannot provide for his son's emotional needs when serious illness or disability forces him to turn in on himself. In one instance, a father suffered irreversible and total paralysis as a result of an accident during surgery that was supposed to have been minor. His son was a teenager at the time, and the two of them had begun sharing experiences that promised to bring them closer together.

> Just before he became crippled, he'd started
> to teach me how to fly a plane. I was getting old
> enough, I suppose—I was 16—and he was teaching
> me on Sundays. We'd done it for just a few weeks
> when he had his accident. I remember he was in
> the hospital for I don't know how long, a long
> time. And then they put him into a rehabilitation
> center, and he spent—I don't know—almost a year
> there.... I was 16 in July; the surgery took place in
> December.

In a tragic role reversal, the son became the father's care-taker. And his father withdrew into himself, spending most of his waking hours tending to his own emotional wounds:

> To this day, he hates being a burden. And it's
> like he punishes us all because of it. He is, in a lot
> of ways, unapproachable. I'd defend him with my
> life. But there's really no personal relationship to
> speak of.

### The Substance-Abusing Father

This father is destructive on many levels. Often dangerous, and therefore frightening, he isolates himself from his son, driving wedges between them every time he gets high or drunk.

Here are the experiences of one man who suffered long-term psychological damage as a result of his father's abuse of alcohol. The man had been a New York City cop for eight years; at the time of our interview, he was divorced and a "dry" alcoholic. For the past several months, he had been living with an 18-year-old girl he met when he was called to her house because her father was beating her. (His own father, a former prison security guard, was 73 at the time of the interview. He still drank.)

> For all intents and purposes I've been on my
> own, so far as any type of parental guidance is con-

cerned, since I was 14, because there were no limitations or restrictions. You were on your own. My
father—I'll be diplomatic and forgiving: I'll say he
was sick, okay? He was an asshole. But he was
sick. I took the brunt of his abuse, and I'll have no
problem when he dies. To me it'll be a relief, because it's one less negative in my life. A tremendous negative.

He went on to tell about a number of incidents that capture what it was like growing up in his family. His mother was
often the victim of her husband's drunken violence.

Mostly, though, she was dragging him off me.
A big, strong guy—six foot, 230 pounds. He worked
20 years with the animals in the prison system, and
he was used to this and he liked it. Incredible as it
sounds, you grew up believing that's pretty much
the norm. I was thinking the other day about the
times he came home drunk. And I would somehow
understand—I was, maybe, six—that he was intoxi-
cated. And I would run and hide under the bed.
And sometimes he would come after me. I remember I was terrified. I'd be under the bed and he'd
be trying to reach me or he'd go get a broom and
try to flush me out from under the bed. And I'd be
like a little squirrel under the bed, trying to get
away. I was terrified. I said, "This fucker'll kill me!"

Of his father's emotional legacy, the man observed:

When I think of my father, I'm tremendously
frustrated at times. And I take it out by physical exercise and sex. I think he screwed up my attitudes
toward relationships. About marriage for sure! I
was very leery about getting married. I think I
made a mistake there! There's so many different
ways he affected my life. The violence factor. I

worry about the temper. I think I have a tremendous capacity to hurt someone, and I've done it
numerous times. I've hurt myself. And I think he's
had a tremendous effect on my life. Tremendous.
More, in many ways, than my mother.

### The Spineless, Nonmasculine Father

This kind of father has been accurately described by Robert
Bly in *Iron John*. He says such a man has had the rawness beaten
out of him by women, the church, and the corporation. He fails
to fulfill his responsibility as a parent and leaves the work of
parenting to his wife. He is uncomfortable with the masculine
in himself. He is reluctant to display aggression, even when appropriate. He is indecisive, lacks intensity, and avoids risks. Such
a father fails utterly to communicate his own values to his son.
He is afraid to provide guidance because he mistakenly confuses
guiding his son with imposing his values on him.

One 35-year-old man's experience is typical of the several
people who spoke with me about this theme:

> My father owned and operated his own
> manufacturing business until it burned down.
> That's when I was about nine. He tried rebuilding,
> but he didn't have the heart to make a go of it the
> second time around. He sold the business and
> retired. He was only in his early 40s. Hasn't
> worked since. The ironic thing is that the business
> burned because he'd been a lousy boss. One of the
> workers was supposed to clean a lot of dust and in-
> flammable stuff from a place where they accumu-
> lated in the factory. He didn't. And my father never
> pushed. So he lost everything.

Asked about his father's behavior at home, this man observed:

> My father is a decent person, but he's not a
> man. I've never seen him speak forcefully to

anyone, even when he should. For instance, for
years he used to call this guy who owed him a lot
of money from when he was in business. He used
to almost beg for the money; it was pathetic to listen to. My mother has really run the show at home
ever since I can remember. She was the one who
really raised us. Meetings at school, shopping for
clothes, talking with us about girlfriends and peer
problems, all the little things—she was there for
them. He was tight-lipped.

My interviewee reported that he is plagued by doubts
about himself.

I used to think when I grew up I'd feel comfortable being a man. And I didn't realize until a
few years ago that I don't. It's as though I've never
grown up. I'm not comfortable with myself!

## Overbearing Fathering

Overbearing fathers are experienced by their sons as intimidating, frightening, and incapable of being satisfied. There
are varieties of this type of parenting: excessively demanding
fathers and tyrannical fathers. Each kind has its own permuta-
tions.

### The Excessively Demanding Father

The excessively demanding father asks for far more than
his son can deliver. He may do so for many reasons. He may
be blindly and unreasonably determined to impose his own
values on the child, without taking into account the child's own
desires or the relevance of the values he wants to convey. He
may simply not have enough experience with children to know
what they are capable of. Finally, he may live through his son's
accomplishments.

*Values-imposing fathers.* One man I interviewed had fallen
in love with a woman who was not Jewish. Raised in a conser-

vative Jewish household, he was supposed to marry a nice Jewish girl. But after graduating from college he met Cynthia, an Irish Catholic. Initially his father accepted the fact that his son was dating a non-Jew. However, as the relationship became more serious, his father became vocal in opposing his son's romantic involvement. When I interviewed the son, he was under extreme pressure. His father had not only refused to accept his son's engagement; he was threatening to disown him entirely if he went ahead with the wedding.

> My father won't even talk with me on the phone right now. He's furious that I would defy him with something like this. My mother tells me he's heartbroken, but I don't see it. All I see is the anger. Actually, I've come to expect this kind of behavior from him. He's always been like a heavy weight on me. I could never get out from under [it]. He chose the college I attended! He chose my major! I look back on that now and I can't believe I let him do it! So this is really the first time in my life I've stood up to him. All along, he's been manipulating and controlling.

*Fathers whose unrealistic expectations stem from their limited experience with children.* Some fathers simply lack experience with youngsters. They may believe that their expectations are in line with their son's capabilities, but these fathers expect the impossible. As a result, the son feels inadequate and incapable of satisfying his father.

> My father was an only child. He married at 42 for the first time. During all those years as a bachelor, he had virtually no contact with children. When I came along, he didn't know how to deal with me. He had no sense of what I could do, but he was eager to have me excel. I remember him trying to teach me stuff I had no interest in and

was totally over my head. I grew up feeling I couldn't satisfy him. On top of that, Dad was a great perfectionist. Nothing I did was ever good enough. So I was frustrated. And what began to happen was, I felt that I couldn't do anything unless it was perfect. And I've grown up that way: everything I do has to be perfect.

*Fathers who live through their sons.* When a father is dissatisfied with his own life and lacks the will to make something more of himself, he may try to gain worth in his own eyes and those of others by living through his son's accomplishments. The results are almost always disastrous.

I interviewed a number of men who were the victims of this kind of overbearing fathering. One man was typical. Forty-two years old when we spoke, he was in excellent physical condition, in part because he spent hours in a gym every week. He told me that his lifelong passion for weight-training and athletics can be traced back to his early childhood. Fathered by a man who was small in stature and extremely self-conscious about it, my interviewee had been pushed from childhood to develop his strength and athletic ability. His accomplishments were a great source of fatherly pride.

I did well in sports, and you could see he really enjoyed it. I remember in particular I used to work out with weights—this is when I was 15, 16 years old. I was really working out a lot and I got to be quite strong. I could lift more than the average kid my age. And Dad used to brag about it as though it was more a reflection on him than of me: "Well, Paul," he used to say to one of his friends, "he goes downstairs and pushes 200 pounds over his head."

This father's tendency to live through his son carried over into other areas as well. For example, my interviewee followed in his father's footsteps and became an expert carpenter and general contractor. He told me about homes he restored.

> I bought two old houses and tore them out
> and fixed them up. I knew that was something
> beyond anybody's belief, so I think that's why I
> wanted to do it. Everybody used to say, "In-
> credible! You bought two houses. You gutted them.
> you did all the plumbing, all the carpentry, all the
> electrical. You did all that? All by yourself?" And I
> said, "Yeah." But to be perfectly honest with you, it
> still wasn't enough. It just wasn't enough. It's com-
> ing to me now, that everything I've tried to do was
> to satisfy him, to meet his okay.

### The Tyrannical Father

The tyrannical father may be physically or psychologically abusive. He engenders tremendous fear, and represents a real danger to his son.

*The physically abusive father.* This man is more than demanding or controlling. He tyrannizes the son by threatening violence against him or others in the family. At least some of the time, he acts on his threats.

One son told me about his father, from whom he'd been estranged for many years. During the interview he remarked that his experience with his father was so negative it would be impossible to recall any incident that was either neutral or positive.

He recalled a typical dinner scene: he was sitting around the kitchen table with both parents. The tension was electric. Father sat with a sneer on his face, listening to rock music that blared from a radio he'd placed on the table. No one spoke.

His earliest memories were of brutal arguments his parents had almost daily. On one occasion—he thought that he was 10 or 11 at the time—he recalled witnessing his father strike his mother:

They'd been struggling with each other, pushing and shoving. She was moving backward and he
kept closing in on her. Finally, he pushed her
against a wall. As she stumbled backward, he
closed the distance between them very aggressively.
She raised her arms to protect her face, and he
struck her shoulders. He pinned her against the
wall with his hip, grabbed her wrists from the front
of her face with his left hand, pulled them down,
and struck her across the face with his right hand.
She was screaming and crying. I told him if he
didn't stop, I was going to call the police.

What I hated most was that I was too small
and too young to help. I remember feeling trapped
and helpless in that house. To this day, I dream of
prisons. When I lost my job a few years ago, the
prison dreams became even more frequent and terrifying. I think I was afraid I'd have to go back
home and live with my parents.

*The psychologically abusive father.* This man belittles and de-
means his son. He relies on guilt, intimidation, and shaming.
He may also manipulate by threatening suicide if he doesn't get
what he wants.

One man told me about his father's ongoing psychological
abuse.

He used to insult all of us all the time. He'd
tease my sister mercilessly about her looks, especially her complexion, which was always a problem.
He'd ride me about my schoolwork, comparing me
all the time to my sister, who did a lot better than
me in school. And his teasing wasn't in fun. He
wanted to make you squirm. He was a bastard.

He told me about his father's manipulations.

He used to have a way of making you feel guilty and inadequate. He'd laugh when we were serious about something, when we talked about things that hurt a lot—friends who had turned on us, whatever.

He went on to talk about one incident when he and his sister decided to defy their father on a particular issue.

I think it was chores around the house or something. We absolutely refused to do them, and even enlisted my mother's cooperation in our conspiracy. There was a major scene. We won, alright, but my father was furious. He didn't say a word to any of us for days. He was in a black mood. Later that same week, he tried to shoot himself in the basement. That's the kind of man he was.

# General Consequences of Ineffective Fathering

Human behavior is very complex, affected by countless variables. The consequences of ineffective fathering can be mitigated by such things as the son's access to other male influences (as I said earlier), the quality of the son's relationship with his mother, and the son's individual temperament.

Nevertheless, when fathering is ineffective, several predictable negative consequences can result. On the following pages, I present four of the most common ones, based on my clinical experience and research. My comments are intended to be suggestive rather than exhaustive or definitive. In the next chapter, more specific consequences, tied to specific varieties of ineffective fathering, will be detailed.

## Self-Esteem

When a man is fathered ineffectively, he has lifelong problems with self-esteem.

The effects of inadequate or overbearing fathering are global: they pervade all aspects of the son's life. He may lack self-confidence in a wide range of situations—from learning new skills to thinking about his sexual attractiveness. He may be quick to give up when confronted with a difficult situation or problem. He may have little faith in his capabilities.

Such a man may lack initiative, discipline, and rigor. He is the student who begins college but does not graduate. He is the home repair enthusiast who begins a project with the best of intentions, but never manages to complete it.

In general, he may be unable to manage his life. He is a pool of unrealized potential, accomplishing with great effort only a fraction of what he's capable of doing.

## Positive Sense of Male Identity

When a man is fathered ineffectively, he lacks a positive sense of male identity.

Usually such a man elects one of two options: he either works very hard to prove he is a man—he is "super-*macho*"; or he is effeminate, never successfully disidentifying with his mother.

### The Man Who Must Prove His Manhood

An ineffectively fathered son may be unconsciously driven to prove his manhood and establish his sense of worth as a man. He often looks outside of himself to do it.

This sort of man may feel a compulsion to succeed, in the conventional sense of the term, to an extreme degree. For example, he may acquire wealth and achieve the trappings of success. Nevertheless, he remains empty inside, always compelled to consummate one more deal, acquire one more property, or enhance his wealth in some other way. Sometimes this need results in behavior that is only questionably legal or downright illegal.

The same need to prove himself may drive such a man to test his sexual prowess. He is the consummate seducer, acquiring lovers with the same passion with which he acquires wealth. Yet such Don Juans can't enjoy a relationship with a sexual partner. Even when in love (which they may not even recognize) and when loved in return (which they often don't recognize either), these men are unable to settle down and cherish the pleasures of a mature union. Instead, they are driven to seduce one more partner, to prove their male potency one more time. In the end, they may well become lonely, embittered men, or men surrounded by lovers yet taking pleasure in none of them. Emptiness is again the prevailing irony.

### The Man Who Never Disidentifies With His Mother

There is a second option open to the man who lacks a firm sense of his male identity. He identifies with his feminine side. In itself, this need not be problematical. But such a man typically rejects his masculine self altogether. He goes to extremes and adopts a sort of stereotypical pseudo-femininity. As a result, he becomes the sort of person who fails to earn the respect or liking of other men. Nor is he appealing to women. Gay or straight, he is insipid and unappealing as a person.

The kind of man I'm talking about here isn't simply a nice person with a healthy balance of masculine and feminine traits; he is vapid and disagreeably sweet—passive, dependent, and timid to a decidedly unhealthy degree.

Having repressed his aggressiveness and ambition, he relies on manipulation and sulking to get what he wants in relationships.

Often such a man remains unnaturally and inappropriately close to his mother. He may not marry at all, becoming instead her spiritual lover. If he does marry, he remains unusually close to his mother. Seemingly caring behavior is carried to an extreme, because this kind of man never fully separates from his mother. (He is the sort of man who will maintain his mother's home or apartment while his own is in shambles.) His misplaced priorities ultimately drive a wedge between him and his wife. It's not unusual to see a downward spiral develop in such cases:

as his wife becomes increasingly disenchanted, he turns to his mother with greater and greater frequency. It's not hard to foresee how the scenario ends.

## Relationship to Authority

When a man is fathered ineffectively, his authority relationships are seriously disturbed.

Both as a subordinate and an authority, this man has serious, lifelong problems. In his relationships with authorities, especially males, he may react inappropriately in a number of ways. He may rebel against authority figures in an adolescent manner. He may be extremely subservient—so much so that he stifles all his initiative and thereby loses his value as an employee; or he may be incapable of accepting criticism or suggestions. It's common for such a man to idealize each new boss for whom he works, only to become disillusioned over time when his unrealistic expectations are disappointed.

Take the case of Alan. He was hired to do the layout for a small-city newspaper. When a new computer system was introduced, Alan was upset. The system didn't work well, and Alan's job became decidedly more complex. Being inventive, he found ways to work around the flaws in the new system. But he was often vocal in his complaints about it.

Alan felt certain that the publisher of the newspaper was "in his corner," although he had no reason for thinking so. One day Alan took it upon himself to call the manager of information systems for the newspaper and chew him out about his lousy computer system. He said that from now on he refused to use the system. The manager was furious and reported the incident to the publisher. In short order, Alan was fired. The young man was shocked and enraged. His rage was directed primarily at his publisher who, as Alan saw it, had failed to support him. What he never realized was that his idealized view of the publisher was completely untested and unrealistic.

When such a man is in the position of authority, he is equally ineffective, because he doesn't know how to lead. For example, he may be unable to set limits, make his expectations clear to his subordinates, and say "no" when appropriate. He may be equally unable to offer encouragement, or to recognize and support genuine effort and good work. This type of person may be unable to set goals or marshall cooperation in reaching them. His sense of responsibility may be confused.

### Problems With Intimate Relationships

When a man is fathered ineffectively, he has lifelong problems establishing intimate relationships with both men and women.

Since he's never been close to a man, he may fear any sort of closeness with male friends. Often, he associates closeness with homosexual inclinations, and may bolt if a relationship with a man becomes warm and caring. He may maintain only the most superficial relationships with male friends, sharing interests such as sports or business. But he never sees male companions as sources of emotional support; he cannot turn to male friends when in need. He remains isolated, even within the contexts of such friendships.

Women are both incomprehensible and vaguely threatening to him. His feelings for his own mother, which are likely ambivalent, affect his reactions to women with whom he becomes involved romantically. He has a real fear of intimacy, and so tends to remain cold and somewhat self-contained in the context of intimate relationships. He engages in something psychologists call protective distancing—the tendency to create emotional distance in order to protect oneself from the dangers associated with being emotionally close to someone.

## To Summarize

In this chapter you've learned why fathers play such a crucial role in the psychological development of their sons. There are two types of ineffective fathering: inadequate and overbearing. Several varieties of each type were explained. The most typical consequences of all forms of ineffective fathering are problems of self-esteem, establishing a positive male identity, dealing with authority relationships, and establishing intimate ties.

## Recommended Reading

Bly, R. (1990) *Iron John: A Book About Men*. Reading, MA: Addison-Wesley.

Campbell, J. (1949) *The Hero With a Thousand Faces*. Princeton, NJ: Princeton University Press.

Corneau, G. (1991) *Absent Fathers, Lost Sons*. Boston: Shambhala.

Eliade, M. (1975) *Rites and Symbols of Initiation*. New York: Harper and Row.

Keen, S. (1991) *Fire in the Belly: On Being a Man*. New York: Bantam Books.

Pruett, K. (1987) *The Nurturing Father: Journey Toward the Complete Man*. New York: Warner Books.

Vogt, G. M., and S. T. Stirridge. (1991) *Like Son, Like Father: Healing the Father-Son Wound in Men's Lives*. New York: Plenum Press.

# 5

# Consequences of Father Failure—Work

When Freud said that the two signs of mental health are the ability to work and the ability to love, he might just as well have been defining the criteria for measuring whether a son has been effectively fathered. His observation points to the two areas of life in which effectively and ineffectively fathered men can most easily be distinguished from one another.

Freud's remark serves as the organizing principle for this and the next chapter of this book, which discuss, respectively, work problems and problems of intimate relationships.

In both working and loving, certain variables operate. For example, one work variable is achievement: a man's behavior falls along a continuum of achievement. At one end of the continuum you find compulsive behavior. The person located at this pole is driven to accomplish, obsessed with success and its symbols. By contrast, a person located at the opposite end of the continuum is characterized by a lack of industry, motivation, and perseverance. Frequently he does not know how to work. He may dream of success, but does not do what he must to reach his goals. (You've probably already inferred that the well-adjusted person—the son who has been effectively fathered—falls somewhere toward the center of the continuum.) Look at the diagram below, which illustrates the relationships just described.

## Variable:
## Achievement

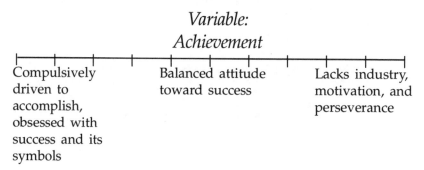

Compulsively driven to accomplish, obsessed with success and its symbols

Balanced attitude toward success

Lacks industry, motivation, and perseverance

This "polar opposites" approach is used for each of the seven variables discussed in this and the next chapter. It is useful for two reasons. First, it makes it easy to predict problems that arise in a son's behavior in the context of work and love; in both contexts, his behavior tends toward the extremes.

Second, this approach makes it possible to account for a paradox: the same kind of ineffective fathering can produce opposite effects, depending on the son's temperament and other factors. For example, a man raised by a father who denigrates his son's talents may be driven to succeed—if only to prove Dad wrong. On the other hand, the son may despair of ever succeeding, essentially accepting Dad's judgment of him as a worthless person unlikely to ever make much of himself. Regardless of which direction the son chooses, he will tend toward one polar extreme or the other.

The well-adjusted son will be neither driven nor overly lax. He will be able to balance his need for success against his desire for a well-rounded life. He will have a realistic appreciation of his talents and weaknesses. Self-acceptance will enable him to adjust to the demands of a particular job or work assignment.

Throughout this chapter and the next one you'll read about examples of sons who fall at one or the other extreme. Inventories will help you determine where your own attitudes and behavior locate you on the continuum. Later in the book you'll learn to reprogram yourself to improve your relationship to work and love.

The four variables to be examined in depth in this chapter are achievement, responsibility, confidence, and authority. In these four areas, the badly fathered son runs into problems in the workplace.

# Achievement

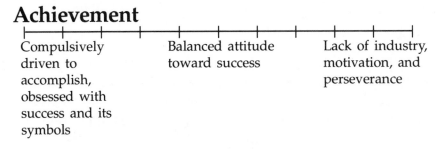

Compulsively driven to accomplish, obsessed with success and its symbols

Balanced attitude toward success

Lack of industry, motivation, and perseverance

### Success Obsession

When Mark took a job with Five-Star corporation, he set out to impress his boss immediately. He volunteered for assignments, worked ten-hour days, and even occasionally came in on Saturdays, when no one else worked. Mark achieved what he sought. His boss was pleased with his industry; before long Mark had been promoted and his salary increased dramatically. In his new position, Mark worked even harder, sometimes spending from 7 a.m. to 7 p.m. in the office. He routinely came in on weekends. He almost always took work home with him. Another promotion soon followed.

With his new-found wealth, Mark bought an enormous home—too big, his wife said, for their needs. He bought two luxury sports cars. He spent money lavishly; his greatest pleasure was showing his acquisitions to friends and relatives, watching their reactions.

Although his wife appreciated Mark's industry and enjoyed the trappings of his success, she was aware that his commitment to Five-Star corporation was excessive. Whenever she spoke with him about it, however, Mark became agitated. It was his career, he said, and he would manage it as he saw fit.

When his wife bore him a baby girl, she hoped Mark would find a better balance in his life. He did not. Instead, he redoubled his commitment to Five-Star. Mother and daughter grew used to eating alone, spending their leisure hours together, even vacationing without Mark. Inevitably, over time, husband and wife began drifting apart emotionally. Right now, Mark's wife is a young, attractive woman with a lovely daughter, and feels as though she's lost her husband to his career.

*Analysis.* Mark's extreme behavior shows a need to prove himself and establish his worth by impressing his superiors and acquiring the symbols of success. His measure of manhood is whether or not a man has won the favor of his superiors and acquired tokens of their approval.

If you were to look into Mark's past, you'd learn that he'd been fathered by a man who was quite successful himself. A corporate vice-president, Mark's father was a cold and rather reserved man who rarely expressed his feelings. (They shook hands when Mark graduated from high school, although, even at that late date, Mark had hoped his father would hug him.) Mark's father was a demanding man, not terribly interested in his two sons. He set high standards for them while remaining emotionally distant. He was arrogant about his own success and made it quite clear to his wife and children that people who have not made it financially are worthy of no serious consideration.

Mark's success obsession can be seen as a reaction to being starved for his father's affection during his childhood and adolescence. In striving to impress his superiors, he is trying to evoke from them the approval and affection he never got from his father. In making his many acquisitions, he is trying to feed his emotional hunger with things. Simultaneously, he is trying to prove himself worthy of his father's notice by making it financially.

## *Inventory:*
## *Does This Sound Like You?*

|  | Yes | No |
|---|---|---|
| You feel compulsively driven to succeed and are unable to find a balance between work and family. |  |  |
| You are hypercompetitive. |  |  |
| You place a great deal of emphasis on acquiring material possessions and take pleasure in broadcasting your success. |  |  |
| Your long hours and commitment to your work cause interpersonal difficulties in your life. |  |  |

## Undermotivation

Office politics is what Jerry hates most. At 38 years old, Jerry has a rather complex and troubled employment history. He's held no fewer than five jobs since graduating college at the age of 26. He was fired from three of them and quit the other two after less than a year.

Jerry is a capable man, but his talent doesn't emerge in the workplace. Typically, he starts a job eagerly; but before long, things begin to turn sour. It's hard to tell which comes first: are Jerry's failures as a worker—his lack of initiative and perseverance, his indecisiveness and tendency to crumble in the face of competition—the start of his superiors' dissatisfaction with him? Or does their lack of appreciation and tendency to play politics result in his losing his motivation, thereby disappointing his superiors? (This latter view is the way Jerry sees it.) Regardless of the answer, things usually end unhappily. Jerry just "doesn't work out" in his position.

After so many unhappy experiences in the workplace, Jerry has all but despaired of ever becoming successful. He has increasingly withdrawn into himself. He doesn't expect satisfaction, nor does he believe that he'll ever be recognized for his work. Sometimes his despair shows itself in his utter refusal to play the game of office politics. At those times, his lack of cooperation is noted by peers and superiors alike. At other times, he behaves as though succeeding didn't matter to him at all.

*Analysis.*  Jerry is stuck. As his employment history suggests, he cannot remain motivated unless he receives constant praise and is exempted from the normal political concerns associated with working with others. (The fact that he did not earn his B.A. until he was 26 is significant: he had a difficult time in college, too. Often, he could not find the discipline and tenacity to complete coursework and fulfill assignments.)

Jerry's family history provides some clues as to why he experiences such severe problems in fulfilling responsibilities and surviving in the world of work. He grew up in a rather strict home. His father was a school superintendent, his mother a teacher. Jerry was one of three siblings, the only boy. Both parents were ambitious people who expected a great deal of their children. During the school year, family life centered around work—the parents' or the children's. Even summers weren't entirely carefree. The father's position was a 12-month one. This meant that family vacations were both short and infrequent. Moreover, Jerry's dad was required to attend board meetings many evenings during the summer.

Jerry felt that he never quite measured up in his father's eyes. His sisters, one older and one several years younger, did better than he in school. His mother and father took great pride in their daughters' accomplishments; Jerry felt like an "also ran."

Though he tried as a youngster to connect with his father, his efforts were unsuccessful. The two never really established common interests.

While still a boy, Jerry began giving up on himself. He became the problem child in the family. Though he never really got into serious trouble, he never quite established himself, either. Much of the anger and resentment Jerry felt toward his parents became unconscious over time. He simply came to feel that he was a failure.

*Inventory:*
*Does This Sound Like You?*

|  | Yes | No |
|---|---|---|
| You never quite feel that you fit in a work environment. |  |  |
| Work is a puzzle: you can't find a way to feel true to yourself while simultaneously learning to satisfy superiors and co-workers. |  |  |
| You feel that you must "sell out" in order to succeed. |  |  |
| You may start a job with excitement, but before long an awful feeling of dread comes over you: the same feelings that posed problems in the past begin emerging again. |  |  |

# Responsibility

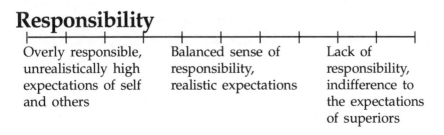

| Overly responsible, unrealistically high expectations of self and others | Balanced sense of responsibility, realistic expectations | Lack of responsibility, indifference to the expectations of superiors |

## Hyperresponsibility

Jose is an assistant professor of English at a large university. Since leaving graduate school and taking his position several months ago, Jose has tried hard to impress his colleagues and department chairman. As director of a basic college-required course in writing, he oversees 12 teaching assistants (TA's) who are working toward their master's degree.

This is Jose's first position in which he must oversee the performance of others. Although he is a bright and eager member of the English department, not all is going well. A number of complaints have come to the attention of the chairman. All indicate that Jose is supervising his teaching assistants entirely too closely and not particularly well. He sits in on their classes more frequently than is required, and often interrupts his subordinates' classes when he feels that the lesson is going badly. For example, if a student asks a question and the TA doesn't answer clearly enough to suit Jose, he interrupts and answers the question himself. This is embarrassing to the TA, and sometimes makes Jose's graduate charges the butt of ridicule.

Other complaints have been made, too. Jose has called frequent meetings of his staff and lectured them repeatedly on the importance of being good role models and maintaining tough grading standards. He has criticized them harshly for minor lapses, such as arriving for class a moment late. An adversarial relationship is beginning to develop, with Jose's subordinates feeling that they can't satisfy him, no matter how hard they try.

*Analysis.* Jose is so eager to prove himself that he tries to control everyone and everything. As a result, he assumes far too much responsibility for events and behavior that he has no need or right to control. This affects other aspects of Jose's life as well. For example, he is maniacal about seeing to it that his children never disappoint their teachers. He even does their homework for them at times.

Jose's problems have a long, complex history. He is the oldest of five children raised in a family in which the father underfunctioned. Often unemployed, he was decidedly not a model of industry, preferring good times to the disciplined caring and hard work that characterize effective fathers. Jose's mother was overwhelmed with the responsibilities of maintaining a household and raising her five youngsters. In addition, her traditional upbringing and lack of formal education limited her options. She could find no work other than a menial job; her meager pay could not even begin to make up for the family's monthly financial shortfalls.

Jose was working by the time he was 14. He took on his shoulders the welfare of his younger siblings. For example, as soon as he was old enough to do so, it was he, and not his father, who monitored the younger children's homework and took responsibility for their progress in school.

Jose's tightly structured personality, his high expectations of himself and others, and his tendency to take over can be traced back to his experiences as a youngster. While these traits served him well during his own schooling (he was an outstanding student), they have become problematical now that Jose must supervise others. His hyperresponsibility is no longer functional.

## *Inventory:*
## *Does This Sound Like You?*

|  | Yes | No |
|---|---|---|
| You distrust human nature and feel that people must be watched very closely and managed aggressively if they are to perform as expected. | | |
| Your life is extremely ordered. Your sense of responsibility is exaggerated, so that you often assume responsibility for solving problems that are not yours at all. | | |
| Others have commented on your tendency to watch them too closely and intrude into matters that are none of your business. | | |
| You have a hard time delegating jobs and sharing responsibility. | | |

## *Hyporesponsibility*

Peter's downfall has always been his lack of responsibility. In some areas of life, this tendency is nothing more than an inconvenience. For example, among his friends he's known as the one who is never on time for social get-togethers; he may even fail to show up at all for dinner appointments made weeks in advance.

But in other areas of life, his lack of responsibility has been more than inconvenient; it's been a source of pain. A woman he loved left him when she found out that he was cheating on her; and yet Peter never really understood why his affairs were such a source of distress to her. He's also lost more than one good job because of absenteeism. Again, Peter thought his bosses unfair for firing him: he was getting his job done even though he might not have been at work as often as his colleagues.

Peter has never really been devastated by the losses his irresponsibility has occasioned. Nor has he felt guilty about his behavior. He is a young 40-year-old, bright, likable, and attractive. So far as he is concerned, it's others, not he, who have the hang-ups over honoring commitments and being on time.

*Analysis.* Peter is not so much outwardly defiant as indifferent to the expectations of others. In this regard, he is a man who has never left adolescence. He has not yet learned that acceptance among adults must be won. Attractiveness, likability, and intelligence may be a ticket to popularity when one is young. They may even win initial acceptance in the workplace. But because long-term success is intimately bound up with fulfilling the expectations of others, Peter may well be in for a rude awakening.

Peter's unrealistic view of the social community can be traced back to his childhood. Peter's father, John, was well into his forties when his only son was born. He adored his son, and throughout his life, worked hard to provide for Peter. He was lavish in his praise of his little boy. He expected very little, but was thrilled at each charming quality or sign of intelligence on his son's part. Peter was never expected to do much to win his father's love. As a youngster, he was assigned few chores. As a teen, he never held a job. Instead, he grew accustomed to having things handed to him.

John set few limits for his son. Curfews, spending ceilings—these were often discussed but never imposed. Consequently, Peter never learned to accept responsibility. Because of his pleasant personality, he was popular with teachers and among his peers. Nevertheless, in school and as an independent adult, the consequences of his distorted view of himself have begun to affect him.

Although Peter still fails to see how he has contributed to his own problems, others can see his failings quite clearly.

## *Inventory:*
## *Does This Sound Like You?*

|  | Yes | No |
|---|---|---|
| You consider yourself a free spirit, bent on experiencing life to the fullest, unwilling to be inhibited by conventional standards of what's right or expected. |  |  |
| It's unfair when others censure you because of their hang-ups about punctuality, absenteeism, and fidelity. |  |  |
| To you, the word *should* is almost always irrelevant (what gives others the right to impose their judgments and expectations on you?). |  |  |
| On several occasions you've run into trouble on the job because you refused to go along with what others felt was proper or appropriate. |  |  |

# Confidence

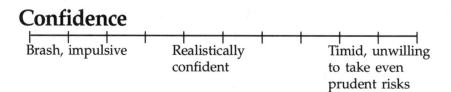

Brash, impulsive          Realistically          Timid, unwilling
                          confident              to take even
                                                 prudent risks

### *Brashness*

Joe has enjoyed tremendous, if fleeting, success in the world of work during his life. An entrepreneur with a gift for sales and marketing, he has launched three different businesses over the last several years. Each was a decided success, at least initially. Joe's powerful personality, and his likability, have done much to inspire the confidence of investors. A bright man, he knows the ropes when it comes to business. He can dazzle potential lenders with compelling data. He can impress with projections. He can even manage to oversee the growth of his businesses during their earliest stages.

But Joe's confidence cuts both ways. He's so confident that he believes he can't fail. He has never developed the discipline required for moderate striving. He is decisive to the point of brashness. He can be impulsive: he rarely weighs the risks of his intended actions, relying instead on bravado and luck to see him through the tight situations he creates for himself.

Although Joe usually enjoys outstanding success during the earliest stages of his business ventures, before long his lack of discipline, his brashness and impulsiveness take their toll, combining to set the stage for eventual failure.

Not surprisingly, he has made and lost hundreds of thousands of dollars during his career as an entrepreneur and investor. Although Joe remains optimistic and confident, with each failure or bankruptcy his track record becomes increasingly questionable.

*Analysis.* Joe's psychological motivation is to prove himself a man by behaving in ways he has come to associate with masculinity: he wants to be tough, unflappable, courageous, definitive, and even arrogant. His view of masculinity is skewed, however, since it's based on media heroes and pop-culture idols.

One key reason why Joe developed such a distorted view of masculinity is that he was raised in a fatherless home. Abandoned by his father while still an infant, Joe never knew the experience of watching a man go through the day-to-day struggles of managing a career and finding his way in life. Joe was an only child raised by a hard-working mother who never remarried—a latchkey kid. Even though he was a superior student, he was understimulated by school. He spent many hours watching TV, going to movies, and reading fantasy novels, which provided the source for his ideal of masculine behavior.

Joe's intelligence and the force of his personality have carried him a long way. However, his business ventures will probably continue to go bust unless he resolves the deep-seated problems resulting from his distorted view of masculinity.

## *Inventory:*
## *Does This Sound Like You?*

|  | Yes | No |
|---|---|---|
| You make impulsive decisions, confident that your intuition, personality, or good luck will see you through. |  |  |
| A measured, reasoned approach to solving problems feels inefficient and alien to you. |  |  |
| Others have faulted you for lacking thoughtfulness and discipline when it comes to planning projects and seeing them through. |  |  |
| Your favorite male heroes are not real people but fictional characters or professional personas you've encountered in literature, film, and the media. |  |  |

### Timidity

Jason often looks back regretfully on his experience as a youngster just out of college. The personal computer industry was just getting off the ground, and this friend Raoul tried hard to convince Jason that there was a lot of money to be made in selling software to PC owners by mail order. Raoul planned to launch just such a business, and he wanted Jason to join him. But Jason was hesitant. Traditional and conservative by nature, he foresaw many potential problems with Raoul's idea. What would happen, he asked himself, if the home computer industry never blossomed as expected? With software changes occurring almost daily, what would happen if they invested in a product line that became obsolete? He shared his hesitations with Raoul;

despite his friend's cogent responses, Jason decided, in the end, to pass. He took a job with his uncle's accounting firm. He has made a decent living. But since the two graduated college, Raoul has become a millionaire.

What troubles Jason most is not the money; it's the fact that his experience with Raoul is in many ways typical of his life. He has often missed out on things, both in work and in relationships, because of his too-timid style. He is really terrified of taking risks. The goals he sets are too modest. He underestimates his capabilities. He has never accurately gauged his attractiveness to women or his abilities as a worker.

*Analysis.*   Jason so fears risk-taking that he has quashed his desire to have an impact on the world, extracting the financial and interpersonal satisfactions he has the right to enjoy. The reasons for this are no mystery.

Jason is the son of a timid and retiring man who was painfully shy, even with family and close friends. On those rare occasions when he tried to exert influence on his children's lives, it was to counsel caution. "Be careful!" was his closing exclamation every time he said goodbye to his children.

By contrast, Jason's mother was, if not overly aggressive, at least solid, influential, and significant in her son's life. Her traditional upbringing made her a person with simple values and a great respect for authority. She saw it as her job to raise her children with the values she had learned. And she did it— principally by taking control of their education and seeing to it that they attended strictly run, first-rate schools all the way through college.

As he was growing up, Jason never truly disidentified with his mother. He assimilated her conservative style of thinking and behavior while co-opting his father's timidity.

*Inventory:*
*Does This Sound Like You?*

|  | Yes | No |
|---|---|---|
| You've let opportunities go by because you could not muster the courage to overcome your discomfort in the face of uncertainty. |  |  |
| People whose judgment you respect have observed that you are sometimes too dependent on the tried-and-true. |  |  |
| All other things being equal, if you were given the choice between a secure job that doesn't pay very well and a more lucrative one that is quite insecure, you would almost certainly choose the secure position. |  |  |

# Authority

Men who have been ineffectively fathered experience much of their difficulty functioning in the workplace around the area of authority relationships. Most such men have never worked through their feelings about the first authority figure in their lives, their father.

The issue of authority relationships in the workplace must be looked at from two perspectives: a man's behavior as an authority, and his behavior as a subordinate.

## *Behavior as an Authority*

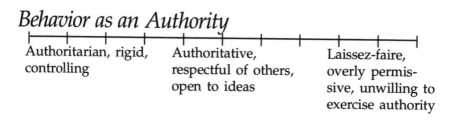

| Authoritarian, rigid, controlling | Authoritative, respectful of others, open to ideas | Laissez-faire, overly permissive, unwilling to exercise authority |

## Authoritarianism

Alan is a junior partner in a large public accounting firm. Young and well-regarded by his superiors, he appears to have a bright future in the company. Since coming on board six years ago, he has established a reputation as a tough, decisive executive. His personal style is abrasive: he is extremely controlled, blunt to the point of rudeness, and frequently relentless in his criticism. He also tends to see things in black and white. He is cold and unfeeling in applying rules, and has virtually no regard for the subordinates whose work he must direct. He believes that people dislike working and have to be threatened with punishment if they are to perform satisfactorily. According to Alan, people lack ambition, want to be told what to do, and prefer taking orders to assuming responsibility.

Though Alan is hated by many of his subordinates, they fear him. He mistakes their fear for respect.

Most of the partners in the firm admire Alan's no-nonsense style of leadership. Others find it objectionable. But almost all of them become uneasy when they see firsthand, as he does not, just how much hostility his style generates among his subordinates. Unlike Alan, they are far from oblivious to the electric tension he creates.

Alan may seem to have a bright future in his public accounting firm. In fact, however, it is only a matter of time before his authoritarian style comes back to haunt him. For in a psychological environment of the type he cultivates, hostility will find its way to the surface. And responding with more controls will only serve to fuel its fires.

*Analysis.* Alan's way of exercising authority is an immature one. His reduction of the world to simple black and white is a clear indicator of the relative simplicity of his moral view of things. So is his emphasis on control: in his view of reality, people must be controlled by whatever means are necessary, or their lazy, irresponsible nature will be reflected in their work.

A guilt-ridden man, he projects onto subordinates much of the irresponsibility of which he feels himself capable. Indeed, some judicious questioning would reveal that Alan lives in fear of being "found out" himself. By controlling subordinates as completely as he does, he is, in fact, controlling himself.

Taking a family history would reveal that Alan was raised by an overbearing, tyranical father who completely dominated his wife. A stern and cruel man, he physically abused Alan and his younger brother throughout much of their childhood. Bitter feelings between Alan and his father were, in fact, the principal reason why Alan left home at 18 and never returned.

## Inventory:
### Does This Sound Like You?

|  | Yes | No |
|---|---|---|
| Most people are lazy and unmotivated. They don't deserve your respect or any special consideration. |  |  |
| Others have commented on your rigidity and closed-mindedness. |  |  |
| At work you place so much emphasis on achieving your goals that you sometimes alienate subordinates. |  |  |
| In most relationships, you have difficulty getting in touch with emotions that might be described as "tender" or "soft." |  |  |

### The Laissez-faire Personality

When Charlie was hired as a chief librarian in a large suburban high school, he was delighted. He'd been teaching for several years before returning to graduate school to earn an advanced degree in library science. Charlie loved children, and he loved books. The opportunity to help youngsters learn to discover the world of books was a source of real joy to him.

Charlie's position had just one drawback for him. He was required to supervise a staff of five female aides, nondegree staff members whose job was to process new books, update the card catalogue, and see to the day-to-day running of the library.

Charlie had never been comfortable in a supervisory position. Except in the classroom, where he was looked up to by students, he disliked being a boss. He felt awkward providing direction, imposing expectations, and exacting discipline when necessary.

Several complicating factors added to Charlie's problem. The staff of aides had been together in the library for several years. The pecking order among them had pretty well been worked out, and their leader was a strong-willed woman who was used to running things in the library as she saw fit (the previous librarian had exercised little real authority). To make things worse, the aides were not pleased with their salaries, and their general attitude was less than cooperative.

Within months of beginning his job, Charlie was encountering serious problems. Students and faculty had begun to complain about the condition of the library and its holdings. Books were not being shelved properly; reference materials were strewn about on tables and some were missing.

Charlie tried hard to respond to these complaints. He issued directives but they were ignored. His staff were superficially pleasant to him but their behavior was oppositional.

Charlie was in a quandary because he felt extraordinarily uncomfortable imposing his will on the library staff. Afraid of exercising real leadership, Charlie saw no way to bring his subordinates into line so that his plans were implemented. The library continued to fall into disarray physically, as tasks were left half-done. The social structure of the system remained essentially unchanged, with Charlie as the nominal leader, while in fact the leader of the aides continued to run the show.

*Analysis.* Charlie can be described as having a laissez-faire approach to the point of being ineffectual. Although he has the academic credentials for his job, he is temperamentally unsuited for it. He lacks the self-esteem necessary to exercise leadership: he is afraid of being disliked or appearing unkind in the eyes of others.

The reasons for his discomfort in the role of leader are many. From his earliest years, Charlie was the peacemaker in his family. Raised by parents who were not happy together, Charlie's home life was filled with strife. The only son and the oldest of three children, Charlie was often drawn into his parents' battles. He learned to placate and pacify, and came to view almost any direct expression of one's will and preferences to be undesirable and contentious.

In the emotional battlefield that was his home, Charlie sided with his mother against his decisive, but harsh and aggressive father. (It was his unhappy home life, in fact, that resulted in Charlie's steeping himself in books as a child.) By the time his father died when Charlie was in his late teens, he had all but eliminated from his personality any traces of his father's decisiveness, harshness, and aggression.

Little wonder that Charlie found his position as leader unbearably painful: it called on him to set goals, to make decisions, to say "no" to subordinates—in short, to do the very things Charlie had come to associate with his father.

## *Inventory:*
## *Does This Sound Like You?*

|  | Yes | No |
|---|---|---|
| You are uncomfortable when called upon to exercise leadership over others. |  |  |
| Being liked is more important to you than being respected. |  |  |
| Others have commented on your lack of assertiveness—for example, your failure to confront others when you're upset with them. |  |  |
| You believe that the exercise of power by one person over another is almost always wrong. |  |  |

# *Behavior as a Subordinate*

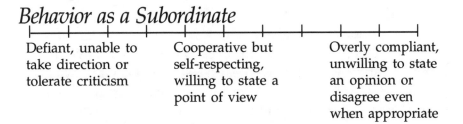

| Defiant, unable to take direction or tolerate criticism | Cooperative but self-respecting, willing to state a point of view | Overly compliant, unwilling to state an opinion or disagree even when appropriate |

## *Defiance*

From the time he was a freshman in high school, Gary has had a rebellious streak. He had serious problems in school, and was branded "defiant" by more than one teacher. Despite his parents' best efforts to talk sense into Gary, he continued his troublesome behavior throughout his high school career. He never went on to college.

His tendency to oppose the direction of superiors has outlived his adolescence. He's lost several jobs because of his unwillingness to take direction. Grounds for his dismissals have ranged from his moodiness and touchiness when he is given instruction and his work performance is criticized to his outright hostility toward supervisors.

Although Gary usually writes off these experiences as proof of his contention that authorities can't be trusted, on a few occasions he has suspected that he may be contributing to his own problem, and he has made some attempts to understand his behavior. On the recommendation of a therapist, he conducted a self-analysis and wrote down the results; but he could only come up with these remarks: (1) I don't trust people with power. (2) I resent being told what to do. (3) If I'm given an order I don't like, and I comply without a fight, I feel like I have no guts.

*Analysis.*   Gary's problems as a subordinate are, indeed, largely of his own making. Evidence can be found in the fact that his overwhelmingly negative and distrustful attitudes toward authority carry over into all authority relationships and have little bearing on the actual person who happens to be Gary's superior at any given time.

A personal history would reveal that Gary has never really come to terms with his overbearing stepfather. Gary was the product of a broken home. After his parents' divorce, which occurred when Gary was eight, his mother remarried. His stepfather was a naval officer, extremely dogmatic and cold. Gary has vivid memories of working hard as a youngster to please his rigid stepfather, but instead of having his efforts rewarded, he recalls an unending stream of criticism and fault-finding. On one occasion, when Gary mowed the lawn of their suburban home, his stepfather actually inspected the job, stepson in tow, pointing out flaws.

Gary remained on cordial terms with his stepfather even after his mother died, perhaps because he never consciously acknowledged his hurt and rage at the man's cold and demanding nature. Gary's hurt, distrust, and rage against authority are displaced feelings left over from his childhood experiences with his stepfather.

## *Inventory:*
## *Does This Sound Like You?*

|  | Yes | No |
|---|---|---|
| You are distrustful of authority, typically seeing the behavior of superiors hidden and harmful motivations. |  |  |
| A directive from a superior places you in an either-or position: either you comply and lose your self-respect or you preserve your self-regard by refusing to go along. |  |  |
| Others have commented on your uncooperative nature. |  |  |
| You are closed to criticism. Most critics are just on an ego trip. |  |  |

### Overcompliance

Since being hired at his new job, Sylvester has performed admirably in almost all respects. He is a terrific employee, gets along well with superiors and co-workers, and is bright, energetic, and cooperative. In fact, he's made it quite clear that he's eager to please his superiors in every way he reasonably can. He is unfailingly courteous, respectful, and diplomatic.

The problem with Sylvester is that he lacks initiative. Although he works hard, he is getting a reputation as a "yes-man." Unwilling to disagree, he seems to have the ability to suspend his own judgments in most situations—even those in which his judgment is important and his input would be valued. He tends to be quite passive, prompting one superior to label him "Silent Sylvester." On those rare occasions when Sylvester has offered an opinion, he has revised his thinking if he senses the slightest opposition to his point of view. He'll do anything to avoid a confrontation.

His unwillingness to question, challenge, and disagree openly has resulted in his good first impression losing some of its luster. People have come to realize that something is missing in this man. Rather than winning their respect, Sylvester has begun to lose it. Instead of being taken seriously and accepted as a valued subordinate and co-worker, he has begun to be discounted and overlooked. Sylvester himself is only aware of his sincere efforts to please, and feels disappointment and resentment that his hard work so often goes unrecognized.

*Analysis.* Sylvester's overcompliance is a long-standing personality trait. He was an intelligent, fun-loving, and boistrous youngster. But his father openly favored Sylvester's older brother, to the point of ignoring Sylvester. He learned that there was little benefit to be gained by being himself—open, enthusiastic, and assertive by nature.

Sylvester has few pleasant memories of his father. He recalls when he was a little boy thinking that he would be willing to do anything to get his father to respond to him. But try as he might, nothing could win the man over.

Eventually, Sylvester gave up. He became a quiet, compliant child in the hope that his passivity would win for him the approval his intelligence and outgoing personality could not. As he matured, his sadness, anxiety, and loneliness became chronic, and his desperate desire to please transformed him from a spunky child to a docile and characterless young adult.

## *Inventory:*
## *Does This Sound Like You?*

|  | Yes | No |
|---|---|---|
| You find confrontation so disagreeable that you would rather go along with something you oppose than be forced to make a scene. |  |  |
| You are expert at rationalization actions you take to satisfy others, often even convincing yourself that you really do want what you know you don't. |  |  |
| You sometimes feel resentful that, despite your best efforts to be liked, others take you for granted and fail to appreciate your talents and hard work. |  |  |
| You've been accused of lacking initiative and obeying blindly when more critical and assertive behavior would be appropriate. |  |  |

In this chapter you've learned about the most important adverse consequences of ineffective fathering on a man's experiences in the work world. A man who has been badly fathered behaves in ways that tend to fall at the extreme ends of the continuum of achievement, responsibility, confidence, and authority. Your inventory results can help you determine the degree to which you suffer from having been ineffectively fathered (the more *yes* answers you gave, the more closely you can identify with this syndrome). By working conscientiously to understand the origins of your extreme behavior and change it for the better, you will almost certainly enjoy your work and work relationships more; you may even find your career taking a turn for the better.

In the next chapter, you'll see that the same tendency to behave in extreme ways characterizes a man's behavior in intimate relationships when he has been ineffectively fathered.

# Recommended Reading

Andersen, C. P. (1983) *Father: The Figure and the Force*. New York: Warner Books.

Cormier, S. (1993) *Am I Normal: Your Personal Guide To Understanding Yourself and Others*. New York: Carroll and Graff Publishers, Inc.

Corneau, G. (1991) *Absent Fathers, Lost Sons*. Boston: Shambhala.

Forward, S. (1989) *Toxic Parents: Overcoming Their Hurtful Legacy and Reclaiming Your Life*. New York: Bantam Books.

Hardy, M., and J. Hough. (1991) *Against the Wall: Men's Reality in a Codependent Culture*. New York: Ballantine Books.

Janov. A. (1972) *The Primal Scream*. New York: Dell Publishing Co.

Keen, S. (1991) *Fire in the Belly: On Being a Man*. New York: Bantam Books.

Miller, S. (1983) *Men and Friendship*. Los Angeles: Jeremy P. Tarcher, Inc.

Osherson, S. (1986) *Finding Our Fathers: How a Man's Life Is Shaped by His Relationship With His Father*. New York: Fawcett-Columbine.

# 6

# Consequences of Father Failure—Love

In this chapter you'll learn about the ways in which a legacy of ineffective fathering shows itself in a man's intimate relationships. (The focus here will be on heterosexual relationships, although it should be borne in mind that virtually all these patterns can be found in relationships between men as well.) The chapter focuses on three key variables: connectedness, emotionality, and pain. For each variable, you should imagine that a continuum exists. The extremes of behavior are located at each end of the continuum. A man's behavior tends toward either extreme if he has been fathered badly. By contrast, a man who has been fathered well acts in ways that fall at or near the midpoint of the continuum.

# Connectedness

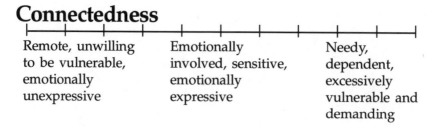

Remote, unwilling
to be vulnerable,
emotionally
unexpressive

Emotionally
involved, sensitive,
emotionally
expressive

Needy,
dependent,
excessively
vulnerable and
demanding

## *Remoteness*

Bob is apparently a successful man. As an innovative director of information services for a large urban hospital, he earns a fine living. He is well respected by his peers and is often a featured speaker at meetings of his professional associations. He has begun to develop a reputation far beyond the narrow confines of the hospital.

But Bob's private life is in shambles. His wife of only five years is woefully unhappy in the marriage. She has told Bob that she wants a divorce. He feels shocked and extraordinarily anxious about his wife's decision, so much so that he's started to experience panic attacks. He's begun seeing a therapist, although he hasn't been able to bring himself to tell his wife that he's in treatment.

In therapy he reveals that he's had a long history of unsuccessful relationships with women. His current marriage is far and away the longest intimate relationship he's ever had.

Because few of his past relationships lasted more than several months, Bob never learned the crucial interpersonal skills of intimate negotiation or communication. This is one of his wife's complaints. She often tells him that she feels like a business associate instead of a wife.

While talking about his wife's dissatisfaction in the marriage, Bob tells his therapist almost in passing that he's been involved regularly with prostitutes ever since graduate school. He justifies his current dalliances as the consequence of his having virtually no sexual relationship with his wife. He glosses over the fact that his involvement with prostitutes predates the current marital crisis by many years. When he is asked to elaborate on his involvement with prostitutes, Bob frankly acknowledges that he enjoys his sexual encounters with them. What he likes especially, he reports, is that they are business transactions; they offer high degrees of predictability which he finds very agreeable. Moreover, they require no emotional vulnerability and no interpersonal entanglements.

Further investigation reveals that Bob has no male friends. The few men he calls friends are in reality business associates who share an interest in software development. When they get together, it is usually around a computer. They talk shop.

By temperament, Bob is aloof and abrasive. His voice and manner have an undercurrent of cold, intellectual sarcasm of which Bob is unaware. He is precise in his choice of words and curt in his manner. He seems to create a distance between himself and others even as he speaks with them. He has no idea of the extent to which he puts people off.

*Analysis.* Although there is a sort of logic to Bob's behavior and the effects it has on his life, the big picture eludes him entirely. As a consequence, the reasons why Bob's professional life is so successful while his private life is a disaster remain a mystery to him.

Bob was raised by a deeply troubled father and a weak, ineffectual mother. He is unhesitating in revealing his utter contempt for his father, whom he calmly describes as "the most vile man who ever lived." He details horror stories of a paranoid, abusive, probably psychotic man who made life a living hell for his wife and only son. Bob's mother was too insecure to leave her husband, so mother and son suffered together.

Not surprisingly, Bob has been estranged from his parents for many years. By the time Bob went off to college, he had come to despise both parents, though some shred of sympathy for his mother remained. He maintains occasional contact with her, but assiduously avoids talking to his father unless absolutely necessary.

Bob's childhood turned him into an emotionally remote man. His love of computers, which developed when he was a youngster, is no accident. Unlike people, computers could be turned on and off, and were not at all threatening. In addition, Bob could apply his substantial intellectual gifts to mastering the intricacies of computer languages. His personal style became extremely, almost absurdly, logical—which served him well in his career but horribly in his interpersonal life.

Bob's capacity for emotional connections with others has been stunted from childhood. Having been hurt so often himself, and having seen his mother suffer as well, Bob learned to be terrified of being close to other people, since he associates being close with feeling hurt and vulnerable. The closest he can come to recognizing that he fears emotional vulnerability is his realization that in dealings with prostitutes he feels safe because their relationships are governed by explicit, businesslike contracts.

If Bob could see the big picture, he might recognize that his interpersonal maneuverings are really ways to keep people at bay. His tone of voice, his physical posturing, and his precise choice of words all suggest that he wants to maintain a safe emotional distance from others.

The fact that Bob's few male friends are business associates is no accident, either. Bob can't be a friend in the usual sense of the word, for friendship implies a lack of structure, even pointlessness. Bob experiences high levels of anxiety in such unstructured situations.

## *Inventory:*
## *Does This Sound Like You?*

|  | Yes | No |
|---|---|---|
| You are uncomfortable in close relationships, because you can't "hide out" emotionally. |  |  |
| Over the years you've developed mechanisms for controlling the distance between you and others. Most of the mechanisms are automatic, but at times you're quite aware of what you're doing. |  |  |
| Most of your friendships are centered around purposeful activities because you find it difficult to be close to people unless you're doing something purposeful together. |  |  |
| At least some of the time, your friends drift away for reasons you can't understand. |  |  |

## *Neediness*

When Ted and Cindy met she was awed by his gentleness. Tender, sensitive, and empathic, Ted seemed charming. Certainly he was the sort of man a woman loves to talk with when she needs a male friend she can trust. She liked the fact that he respected her and went out of his way to take her feelings and needs into account. The early stages of their relationship were immensely satisfying for both of them.

Almost a year into the friendship, however, things began to go badly. Ted began to display traits that had not been apparent earlier. Cindy learned that in return for his tender affection he expected her to fulfill his completely unreasonable emotional demands. For example, she was expected to gloss over any annoying behavior on Ted's part and to always be unstinting in her praise even if she felt disapproving. If she criticized

Ted in any way, she ran the risk of plunging him into a pro-tracted funk. Ted discouraged her from forming friendships of her own, as he felt threatened by them.

In exchange for his warmth and openness, Ted expected to have his overwhelming dependency needs met. Cindy was expected to shore him up constantly, providing reassurance and bolstering his ego. She also had the job of protecting him from people he didn't want to deal with by running interference for him on the phone and at social gatherings.

Finally, in return for his sensitivity, he expected uncondi-tional forgiveness each time he sulked or carried on like a spoiled child.

Unknown to Cindy during the early stages of their rela-tionship, Ted had certain traits that also contributed to his hav-ing serious problems in the business world. Some of these traits were relatively minor. He had a limp handshake and avoided eye contact when he spoke with men. He was rather small-minded and petty in his concerns, placing emphasis on symbols of status rather than on matters of substance. For example, once he railed on and on about how a colleague had been given a plaque at work; Ted felt that he should have been the one who received the boss's mark of approval.

Other traits were more serious. Ted tended to be passive and unreliable. These traits led to the loss of one job that pre-dated his relationship with Cindy. His inability to accept criti-cism had contributed to the loss of another. He was rarely asser-tive. When others disappointed or upset him, in the workplace or elsewhere, he did not confront them. Instead, he sulked. He could be passive-aggressive. When others displeased him, he got even by failing to keep promises and not following through on agreements.

*Analysis.* Ted's passivity, unreasonable emotional de-mands, dependency, and extreme neediness have had the long-term effect of alienating others. Over time, the women he attracts lose respect for him and come to despise him. He is often deeply hurt by the fact that they "turn on him"—his words—after he has done so much for them. What he does not know is that his personal style is extremely off-putting.

Ted has not found a way to express himself as a person or as a man, or to trust that he will be accepted. He fears rejection to such a degree that he goes out of his way to hide his faults by cultivating his heightened sensitivity and compassion. However, because he is human, and because he has potentially disagreeable feelings and needs, Ted cannot long keep his dark side hidden from view or himself immune from criticism. The other or objectionable side of him—his aggression, for example—makes its way to the surface in the form of extreme emotional demands on others, sulking, and passive-aggressive behavior. Ted is completely oblivious to the emotional demands he makes on others. So far as he is concerned, there is nothing in his day-to-day dealings with people that can account for their losing respect for him.

Ted's problem was contributed to in large measure by the fact that his father was an emotionally constricted man. The father had a problem similar to Ted's. He lacked the spunk to wrest from life the satisfactions he wanted. He held a low-paying, low-status job, and was quite dissatisfied with his own life. At home, he lacked the courage to disagree with his wife or assert his own needs when it was appropriate to do so. As a result, he was quite depressed and more than a little hostile, but not overtly. His hostility showed itself in a lack of involvement with his wife and son. He was detached and sullen.

Ted never quite disidentified with his lonely and unfulfilled mother, who lacked the education or resources to make a life apart from her husband. As Ted grew older, he became his mother's emotional companion. This is why he has such a keen sense of women's needs in relationships. He learned well to care for and nurture women, at least in a superficial way, because this behavior was an immense source of satisfaction for both him and his mom. He also took on many of his mother's traits—emotional expressiveness, dependency, and sensitivity.

Ted lacked a model upon which to base his behavior as a man, so he chose to bury his specifically male orientation. For example, he denied and repressed his aggression. Of course, it never disappeared; it simply went underground in Ted's personality. Thus, it shows itself in his subtle but extreme emotional demands, his passive-aggression, and his manipulativeness.

### Inventory:
### Does This Sound Like You?

|  | Yes | No |
|---|---|---|
| You are more comfortable around women than men. |  |  |
| Women find you desirable initially, but they lose interest over time. |  |  |
| You are often dissatisfied because others don't show you the respect you want, but you are unable to find a remedy. |  |  |
| When you are frustrated or hurt, your automatic response is to withdraw. You hope to elicit tender, loving care from the people close to you without having to ask for it. When this fails to happen, you punish them by withdrawing even more and sulking. |  |  |

# Emotionality

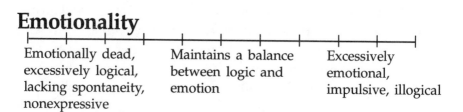

| Emotionally dead, excessively logical, lacking spontaneity, nonexpressive | Maintains a balance between logic and emotion | Excessively emotional, impulsive, illogical |

## Hypoemotionality

Ian's career is ideally suited to him. A laboratory researcher for a pharmaceutical company, he spends most of his work week designing and implementing scientific studies to test the efficacy of various natural and synthetic chemical compounds. His meticulous work has won him warm praise and generous financial recognition.

By temperament, Ian is a reserved, quiet person. Thoughtful, deliberate, and extremely logical in his approach toward life, in many ways he resembles the typical "head-in-the-clouds" researcher. He is the sort of person who almost never responds spontaneously to any event. In conversation, there is a lag before Ian responds, as he carefully formulates what he wants to say.

It's no accident that Ian spends most of his work week working alone or with only a few other people. His interpersonal life leaves much to be desired. He has few friends, and his relationships with his intimates are strained and awkward.

Ian's wife, his third, was attracted to him by his intelligence and emotional self-control. But Myra never anticipated that Ian's cold, affectless style would not ease somewhat as the intimacy between them grew. It never did. Rather than becoming more relaxed and spontaneous, Ian has retained his hard, rigid, and logical style. This is a source of extreme distress to Myra. Her distress is heightened when she observes her husband interacting with their baby daughter. Though she knows that Ian cares for the baby, he is almost never physically or emotionally expressive with her.

Ian and Myra have talked a great deal about how he can loosen up, become more spontaneous, put logic aside, and relax. Try as he might, however, Ian has not changed. His approach to everything, from balancing the family budget to responding to his mother-in-law's serious illness, is invariably logical and reserved.

At this point, their relationship is in jeopardy. Myra has brought up the subject of divorce, saying that she finds Ian's extreme even-temperedness and lack of expressiveness unbearable. In characteristic fashion, he responded to her by logically evaluating the pros and cons of ending the marriage. The logic of his response made Myra feel even more rejected and emotionally abandoned.

*Analysis.* It's no accident that Ian has become wedded to logic and has all but lost contact with his emotions. Emotional withdrawal was a lesson Ian learned as a child. Both Ian's parents were demanding but emotionally inhibited people. Ian modeled his behavior on that of two people who were utterly lacking in spontaneity and viewed all emotional expression as dangerous and undesirable.

As a result, Ian learned to keep his spontaneous emotional reactions in check. He prided himself on his logic and the fact that his emotions would never run amok.

This style served Ian well at school, and it is also an asset in his career. However, it has been disastrous in his personal life. Yet he remains unwilling—perhaps at this point unable—to change.

## Inventory:
## Does This Sound Like You?

|  | Yes | No |
|---|---|---|
| Control of your emotions is of primary importance to you. |  |  |
| You distrust spontaneity. |  |  |
| You prefer a logical approach to life's problems. |  |  |
| When you have been in situations that are inherently emotional (attending a funeral, for example), you have sometimes been unable to feel anything. |  |  |
| People close to you have told you that they find your self-control to be exasperating. |  |  |

## Hyperemotionality

Ralph has been attracted to an acting career since he was a child. Theatrical performance affords him an opportunity to experience the entire range of intense emotions he craves.

Perhaps not coincidentally, for the past two years, Ralph has been experimenting with drugs of various kinds, from marijuana to cocaine. These substances, too, enable him to run the emotional gamut. To Ralph, suffering and ecstasy are equally stimulating.

Ralph's private life is also intense. His relationships rarely last more than several months, and even his longest-term ties have been emotionally volatile; terminations, reconciliations, and negotiations occur with tedious regularity. One woman captured an important truth when she accused Ralph of managing his private life as if it were a drama being played out for an audience.

Ralph craves constant love and attention. He is emotionally sensitive and vulnerable, disorganized, hysterical, and illogical. His tenderness and emotional spontaneity are appealing to women initially, but these traits become wearing in time, much to his distress.

*Analysis.* Ralph is a "feeling junkie." He doesn't feel alive unless some strong emotion is coursing through his body. Unconsciously, he maneuvers himself and other people into situations that evoke intense feelings.

His hunger for feeling can be traced back to childhood. Even as a tot, Ralph sought out stimulating experiences, heedless of any risks of injury to himself. He rode his bicycle recklessly; later, as a teen, he was repeatedly ticketed for speeding, reckless driving, and an array of less serious traffic offenses. For as long as anyone could remember, Ralph was the sort of person who wanted to experience life "on the edge."

Although this tendency was to a great degree inborn, it was also a function of his relationship with his father, an emotionally remote man whom Ralph simultaneously adored, feared, and despised. An ambitious tradesman, Ralph's father maintained only a peripheral emotional tie with his wife and son. Physically strong, he was an impressive man who was able to earn a very good living and provide well for his family. But he was always a mystery to Ralph. His father offered just enough attention and involvement to stimulate the boy's curiosity and admiration. Father and son shared very little time together and even fewer interests.

Ralph's fear of his father can be traced back to the punishments he received as a result of his misbehavior. His father could not understand his overactive, impulsive, and irresponsible son. On a few occasions, usually when Ralph had run-ins with school administrators and law enforcement officials, his father pummelled him.

Ralph's dislike of his father grew over time. In retrospect it became apparent to him that his dad had escaped into his work during most of Ralph's childhood. Ralph's impulsive and irresponsible behavior was motivated in part by his desire to involve his father in family matters more than he otherwise would have been.

Ralph's interest in theatre was largely a function of his innate craving for stimulation; but his complex and fundamentally unsatisfying relationship with his father also entered into it. A popular and unconventional high school drama coach saw a spark in Ralph and sensed his hunger for a father figure. He became a surrogate father to the boy; the two spoke and shared more than Ralph and his father ever had. When the coach involved his pupil in a production of "Death of a Salesman," casting him as Biff, the young boy was hooked. Theatre became a way for Ralph to satisfy his need for stimulation while affording him many opportunities to come to grips with his mixed feelings toward his father.

## *Inventory:*
## *Does This Sound Like You?*

|  | Yes | No |
|---|---|---|
| If you're not feeling some intense emotion, life seems bland and uninteresting. |  |  |
| Your close relationships are tumultuous, vacillating between such emotional extremes as love and hate, and ecstasy and despair. |  |  |
| To be without the love and attention of those you care for is more than painful to you; it drives you to extremes of behavior in order to elicit the reactions you crave. |  |  |
| Many of your relationships start off passionately, but in time they become sources of pain and distress; almost all your relationships end unhappily. |  |  |

# Pain

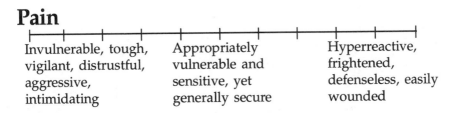

| Invulnerable, tough, vigilant, distrustful, aggressive, intimidating | Appropriately vulnerable and sensitive, yet generally secure | Hyperreactive, frightened, defenseless, easily wounded |

## *Invulnerability*

Andy has long had a reputation for being tough. As far back as high school, he's been known as a scrapper. He is not one to be threatened by dangerous, potentially hurtful situations. In fact, he seems to seek them out. In much the same way, he relishes and even provokes conflict in his intimate relationships.

To Andy, the world is an adversary. He trusts very few people, and remains vigilant at all times, believing that others will let him down. Even worse, he anticipates that others he considers to be friends may turn on him as enemies. Consequently, he never allows himself to be close to people, and he is always defensive in his personal relationships.

It was his very toughness that made him attractive to Blair. She correctly intuited that beneath Andy's aggressive exterior is a deeply wounded man. As the oldest of five children of an angry father, Blair has been a nurturer from her earliest years. Her fantasy was that she could soothe Andy's hurt and help him discover his capacity for love.

It hasn't worked out that way. Rather than taking away Andy's pain, Blair has become his victim. Although he rarely has been physically abusive to her, the threat is always present in their relationship. He is loud and intimidating. He abuses Blair psychologically, teasing her cruelly and constantly finding fault with her. He undermines her confidence in herself.

Despite her disappointment and her sadness, Blair hangs on, hoping that she will one day be able to lead Andy out of the despair she knows he experiences every day of his life. She maintains a stubborn determination to heal the hurts of her own past by changing Andy.

*Analysis.* Blair's optimism is misguided; she is hoping for a miracle.

Without long-term help, it's unlikely that Andy will ever break out of his dysfunctional behavior pattern. No simple loving relationship, no woman—no matter how caring, how patient—will be able to break through the defenses Andy has set up.

He is, indeed, deeply wounded. The reasons are many. For one, Andy's father abandoned the family when Andy was six. Andy has never gotten over the hurt. He still remembers his father.

Andy's alcoholic mother resented her son, seeing in him physical features reflections of the man who'd abandoned her. In her drunken rages she more than once blamed Andy for his father's leaving. She had a long series of lovers, many of them live-ins, who did their best to ignore Andy or frighten him. Once, when he was ten, he was sexually molested by one of them.

Andy learned early on to be tough and wary. He swallowed his pain, hiding it beneath an aggressive exterior. He has learned to trust no one, since the two people closest to him as a child left such deep scars. His hypermasculinity is protective. His ability to absorb pain not only fosters the illusion of his invulnerability, it's also a way of expiating the guilt Andy feels at having driven his father away.

It's not difficult to predict how the relationship with Blair will turn out. If she gets help, she may be able to save herself by leaving Andy. If she doesn't, the pattern of abuse will likely escalate; Blair's physical safety and health will be in danger.

For Andy, healing can only come when he confronts the emotional devastation that resulted from his rejection by both parents. He must see his tough exterior as a little boy's defense against fear and hurt.

## Inventory:
## Does This Sound Like You?

|  | Yes | No |
|---|---|---|
| Your wariness of others makes it extremely difficult for you to form close relationships. |  |  |
| By any number of means—chief among them your aggressiveness—you create emotional distance between yourself and others. |  |  |
| You seek out conflict in your relationships with women. Once you have provoked conflict, you feel an impulse to humiliate, intimidate, and even abuse the woman closest to you. |  |  |
| Most women who are drawn to you are rescuers. Their aim seems to be to heal you through their love. |  |  |

## Hyperreactivity

It's amazing that David ever graduated from college. He is extremely anxious, experiencing a wide range of phobic symptoms—from pounding heart to panic attacks—in response to stresses that most people would consider normal. He avoids driving on freeways, sometimes going miles out of his way in order to stay on smaller, back roads. He is a hypochondriac, beset almost continually by any number of mysterious ailments; he spends more time in doctors' offices in a month than most people log in a year. He is unable to deal with criticism, getting severely depressed when criticized.

David almost always feels that he is at risk of being hurt in some way. He plans many of his activities around not being exposed or vulnerable. He avoids conflict, since he feels defenseless and weak. He does not assert himself, convinced that he lacks the skill to make his wants clear to others or stand up to others in the face of disagreement. He avoids emotional engagement with friends and associates, largely because he doubts their goodwill.

David is attractive and his temperament evokes sympathy from women who believe they can heal his wounds by love. Though many lose patience quickly, a few women have persisted in trying to get through to him. None have succeeded. In the end, they find his self-absorption to be a turn-off.

*Analysis.* Andy and David are more alike than appears on the surface. Moreover, the origins of their pain are strikingly similar. Both are trying to avoid pain, although the means by which they do so are different.

David's father also abandoned the family when David was a child. In his case, mother was not so much rejecting as depressed and anxious. Whereas the hostility of Andy's mother toward her son was overt, David's mother was over-solicitous. She worried about him constantly, confusing worry with love. It was from her that David learned to be anxious, fixate on his health, and become hyperreactive to pain.

David's profound distrust of people—indeed, of life it-self—can be traced to his father's abandonment of the family. The distrust was compounded by the anxiety he learned to experience from his mother's treatment of him.

## Inventory:
## Does This Sound Like You?

|  | Yes | No |
| --- | --- | --- |
| You are often anxious, worrying about your health and spending considerable energy managing anxiety symptoms—such as rapid heartbeat and shortness of breath—that threaten to remove you from the mainstream of life. |  |  |
| You are intolerant of criticism, often feeling hurt when you are criticized. Your feelings are so strong that the content of the criticism doesn't come through, just the fact that you're being criticized. |  |  |
| On more than a few occasions, you've avoided situations that would place you in a vulnerable position. (For example, you may have avoided taking certain courses or going for a job interview.) |  |  |
| In your close relationships, you have trouble asserting yourself or facing out a confrontation. Instead, when conflict arises, you tend to leave. You've often rationalized your decision by blaming your partner for starting a fight. |  |  |

In this chapter you've seen examples of the most important ways in which ineffective fathering affects a man's intimate relationships. Consequences can be seen in a man's ability to connect with a partner and to deal with emotions in a relationship. The consequences of ineffective fathering are also evident in the ways in which a man reacts to pain and inflicts it in a relationship.

The next three chapters focus on making things better. Chapter 7 concentrates on improving your relationship with your father. Chapter 8 shows you how to resolve your feelings about your relationship with an absent father. Chapter 9 provides specific techniques which can help you overcome the adverse consequences of ineffective fathering.

# Recommended Reading

Cormier, S. (1993) *Am I Normal: Your Personal Guide to Understanding Yourself and Others*. New York: Carroll and Graff Publishers, Inc.

Corneau, G. (1991) *Absent Fathers, Lost Sons*. Boston: Shambhala.

Forward. S. (1989) *Toxic Parents: Overcoming Their Hurtful Legacy and Reclaiming Your Life*. New York: Bantam Books.

Janov, A. (1972) *The Primal Scream*. New York: Dell Publishing Co.

Osherson, S. (1986) *Finding Our Fathers: How a Man's Life Is Shaped by His Relationship With His Father*. New York: Fawcett Columbine.

# 7

# Making Peace With Father

Coming to terms with your father—no matter how benevolent, malevolent, distant, or overbearing he was—is in your best interest. For your own success and comfort, you must make peace.

Fortunately, this task can be accomplished whether your father is dead or alive, present or absent from your life. This chapter will show you how. It is divided into four parts. In the first, you'll see why making peace is essential. In the second, you'll learn about the three most important obstacles to that process. Specific techniques are presented in the third. And the fourth provides a series of dos and don'ts, each intended to help you steer clear of the blunders men most often make in their attempts to come to terms with their fathers.

# What Happens When You Fail To Make Peace With Father

If you don't come to terms with your father, you may remain preoccupied with his failings at the expense of your own potential for happiness and success.

One 39-year-old man I interviewed could not talk for more than several minutes at a time on any subject without bringing up his father. He'd compiled a mental list of his father's sins, and was quick to trot it out at the slightest provocation. When he spoke of his father, anger seemed to emanate from every pore of his body.

As a result of the failure to make peace with father, your unresolved negative feelings may undermine your confidence in yourself and diminish the pleasure you can take in your accomplishments and successes. Instead of feeling pleased and satisfied with your development as a person, you feel powerless like a child.

"I don't know why, but I almost never feel like I've grown up," wrote one man. "I'm successful by objective standards—I'm almost 42, but I still feel like a kid." His father, as it turns out, had never acknowledged this man's capabilities, and undermined his confidence continually. He was like a building without a solid foundation: always shaky and ungrounded.

Unresolved feelings about your father may cause you lifelong difficulties forming balanced, mature, and satisfying relationships in every area of your life. Whether with your spouse, children, workmates, superiors, or lovers, your relationships are strained and uncomfortable. You may feel convinced that no one can be trusted, or that no one is quite up to par as a person.

One of my clients told me that he'd tried therapy several times before, but had left each time after only a few sessions. His reasons were varied: one therapist had failed to listen attentively enough. Another was careless about beginning sessions on time. A third seemed untrustworthy. In each case, the therapist demonstrated (to this client's satisfaction, at least) that he was unworthy of the man's commitment. Discussion revealed that a tendency to make unrealistic demands on others pervaded his life experience; the unhappiness that resulted was, indeed, one of the reasons he had sought treatment.

Unless you make peace with your father, old childhood feelings of weakness, powerlessness, dependency, and worthlessness may terrorize or immobilize you. Never far from your mind is the fear associated with not being able to function as a competent adult.

Among men, performance anxiety in both love and work is common. One man in his mid-thirties came to treatment because he'd been promoted at work to a job that involved expanded responsibilities. Although he possessed the training and skill to succeed in his new position, he was convinced that he could not carry it off. A profound lack of self-confidence, which had been kept in check as long as his job demanded relatively little of him, began eating away at him. He was so convinced that he wouldn't be able to perform adequately in his new position that he was thinking about leaving the company.

Your current authority relationships may reflect your failure to come to terms with father, as you continually and unconsciously try to "make things right" between the two of you. Efforts to work out past problems in the present are always doomed to failure.

When a man enters adulthood without having resolved important issues with his father, he is very likely to try to resolve them in his dealings with others—with men in general and male authority figures in particular. He seeks substitute gratifications for the satisfactions he was denied as a child. For example, he'll angrily resist the suggestions of his boss when in fact it's his father toward whom his anger and opposition are really directed. In cases like this, opposing the boss is a symbolic way of acting out your anger at your father; but because it is only symbolic, the need that motivates your anger remains unmet. The process is therefore repeated, but each time real satisfaction eludes you.

Perhaps worst of all, you may unconsciously re-create in your relationships with your children the very same negative patterns that shaped you as a child. A lack of resolution can be very expensive indeed.

One 63-year-old man wrote to me, "I've found I'm much more like my father than I would ever admit when I was young." He went on to say that he often found himself treating his two sons just as his father had treated him. Despite his best efforts to be unlike his father, he was following in his footsteps almost exactly. "I feel like there's some force pushing me along," he wrote, "as though I can't avoid being the very kind of father I promised not to be."

For the reasons just discussed, and also in light of the problems in working and loving detailed in the previous two chapters, it is extremely important that you make peace with your father. But doing so involves more than simply making a decision to proceed. Three crucial obstacles stand between you and what you need to accomplish. These are the focus of the next section of the chapter.

## Obstacles to Coming to Grips With Your Father

If making peace with father were a simple and straightforward task, most men would accomplish it successfully. But it's hardly simple or straightforward—which is why most men enter adulthood with a great deal of "father baggage," unresolved feelings that affect every aspect of their lives.

There are three reasons why men have such difficulty. One is that seeing your father as he truly is and accepting him as a flawed human being is painful and difficult. The second is that most sons carry around a significant burden of guilt toward their fathers. The guilt stems largely from their having formed a silent alliance with mother that had the effect of excluding father from the emotional life of the family. Finally, many sons doubt their father's ability to tolerate attempts to be open and establish an intimate father-son relationship.

## It's Difficult To Accept Your Father as a Flawed Person

All little boys want to believe that their father is perfect: strong, loving, intelligent, successful, and emotionally intact. They take a narcissistic pride in Daddy's accomplishments, personality, and strength. "My daddy is smarter [or stronger or better] than your daddy" is a remark that almost all little boys have made at one time or another—usually to a male playmate with whom they have a competitive relationship.

For much of their young lives, sons cling to their belief in father's superiority. Sometimes doing so requires that they ignore obvious facts. Perhaps father drinks. Perhaps he is nasty and abusive. Perhaps he can't hold a job. In such cases, the young son typically excuses his father, blaming others—sometimes even himself—for his father's failings.

During adolescence, sons challenge their father incessantly. They may balk at his restrictiveness and mock his old-fashioned ways. They test him repeatedly, behaving disrespectfully and provocatively. Nevertheless, in most cases, beneath their behavior is a profound regard for the man. Despite everything they do that seems to suggest the opposite, adolescents want their father to be strong and to stand up to their challenges. They need to know that their father will not crumble: if he lets them down, they will frequently react with anxiety and even dread, since they are now without the limits they were counting on him to set.

It's very important for sons to believe in the invincibility and perfection of their father; and they're often unwilling to surrender their illusions if father is less than perfect. This is one reason why sons often reduce fathers to stereotypes, such as the long-suffering father (see Chapter 3), and why they consider him more often as a symbol and a force rather than as an individual.

Since it's so hard for sons to accept father as a person, forgive him his mistakes and failings, and empathize with his pain, some sons never get beyond an idealized view of him. Those who do may experience a profound sense of grief and loss—the same sense of loss that comes with having to surrender any fantasy. Rather than accepting him as just a man, they hide their grief behind a wall of anger. In many ways it's easier for a son to be angry with his father than to accept him as an imperfect human being.

## Sons May Feel Guilt at Having Formed an Exclusionary Alliance With Mother

Sons and mothers often form alliances that have the net effect of excluding father from the emotional life of the family. There are many reasons for this phenomenon.

Mother, by nature more emotionally attuned to the son, is the more likely candidate for a child's confidante. Presuming that father behaves in ways that are consistent with his cultural conditioning, he is less likely to be equipped for emotional give-and-take. The mother may be hungry for someone—especially a not-yet-tainted male—to listen to her and provide emotional companionship; her son serves this purpose well. This mother-son alliance enables the father to remain emotionally distant from both of them and maintain his detached role while simultaneously hiding from his own feelings. Thus it serves his needs as well as those of mother and son.

Nevertheless, sons know they have silently conspired with mother to exclude father. The guilt they feel about having done so makes the situation even more difficult. This can have an impact on any attempts they may make to converse on a meaningful level with their father later on.

## Sons May Doubt Father's Ability To Tolerate Closeness to Them

Asked what keeps them from forming closer ties with their father, many sons express doubt at his ability to tolerate emotional intimacy with them. Many sons would rather keep their distance than risk rejection from their father.

Although this fear is often misguided—it's been my experience that many fathers are hungry for real contact with their sons—it is very strong. Based on years of seeing their father avoid strong feelings other than anger, sons may fear that the father edifice will crumble in the face of soft, tender, or otherwise "feminine" emotions.

# Techniques

Coming to terms with your father is a long-term process. I don't want to mislead you into thinking that application of the techniques presented below will resolve your relationship for you. Instead, you should view these techniques as facilitators: they make reconciliation possible; they lay the groundwork for it, but they can't guarantee it. Like all self-help techniques, they are only as good and useful as the effort applied to them. Goodwill, sincerity, and self-awareness must be at the heart of any attempt to come to terms with your father.

If you've carefully read the preceding chapters of this book, especially the first three, you're already on your way to making peace with your father. By taking the time to understand why the father-son relationship is problematical (Chapter 1), as well as the kinds of influence your father exerted and the way he did so (Chapters 2 and 3), you've gained important insights that will dramatically increase the likelihood of healing your relationship with your dad.

## Know Your Goals

When you think of coming to grips with your father, you should think in terms both of a general goal and one or more specific ones. The ultimate goal of all your efforts is to let go of your father so that you can live your own life as an independent and mature man. No son has ever become an individual without separating psychologically from the man who gave him life. One step that's essential in moving toward that destination is understanding and accepting him as a flawed human being, to forgive him his mistakes, and empathize with his pain.

Because sons' experiences are so varied, your specific goals will likely be different from anyone else's. Take these three examples:

- If you had a very flawed relationship with your father—if you were abused, abandoned, or otherwise wounded by him—then your specific goal is to free yourself from your anger and resentment. If you fail to let go of the bitterness, your life will be lived out in a sort of trance state, with all your perceptions and reactions colored and shaped by your negative feelings toward your father.

- If you were engaged in a running battle with your dad—if your relationship was characterized by ongoing conflicts and deep differences—your specific goal is to resolve those differences and conflicts and find areas of commonality. If this is for one reason or another impossible, your goal would be to accept the differences between you, understand their origins, and disengage emotionally. Ongoing battles have a way of draining energy and distorting your life experience.

- If you remain an ill-defined person because your loving but intrusive father denied you the opportunity to discover your own preferences and become an individual in you own right, then your specific goal is to step away from your dad, leave his orbit, and break his spell. This requires that you view yourself and your father as objectively as possible and identify the differences between you. The next step is to accept and take possession of those traits, needs, feelings, and wants that are uniquely yours.

## Two Prerequisites

You must meet two prerequisites before you can make peace with your father. First, you need to know that coming to terms with him does not mean minimizing or denying any pain he caused you, or any destruction he brought about. Quite the contrary—you must openly acknowledge his harmfulness.

One man I treated spent many months sidestepping the issue of his father's influence. It seemed clear to me that he must be dealing with internal conflicts that stemmed from his relationship with his father, since telltale signs showed themselves in the man's work history and intimate relationships. Nevertheless, each time I broached the subject, he deftly skirted the issue. "My father's always been the kind of dad every kid wants: encouraging, loving, and sharp. We used to do lots of things together. I don't think he ever missed a baseball game I pitched." On and on went his litany of cheers for Dad. The man idealized his father, held him in awe, and so refused even to consider whether some of father's influence might have been negative.

In passing, one day he mentioned that his father used to drink quite often, but never to excess. Over the next several weeks, when opportunities arose to explore the matter, I pressed the issue. A picture began to emerge of a father who relied on alcohol to maintain his positive moods, cope with his disappointment about his career, and keep his wife at an acceptable distance. He was an episodic alcoholic, not a fall-down drunk; nevertheless, his abuse of alcohol exerted a major influence on every member of this family. As it turned out, the son was on more than one occasion humiliated by his father's behavior. As a result, he was vaguely afraid of his father, felt sorry for him, wanted to respect him, but despised him.

Only when my client could acknowledge these feelings was it possible for him to begin addressing his actual relationship with his father. Progress in therapy was then possible. Changes in the son's behavior, both on the job and in his intimate relationships, followed soon afterward.

The second prerequisite for progress is this: coming to terms with Dad may require that you reframe past experiences. This means being willing to see the good in the bad. For example, one son told the story of a father who was irresponsible and uninvolved in the family. While not denying these truths or their negative aspects, the son was able to realize that some good came of them, too. "My father's unreliability forced me to become independent and resourceful as a kid. It hurt then, and I hated him; but, in a weird way, it prepared me for being an adult."

## The Techniques

There are three things you need to know about the techniques presented on the following pages. First, they will be useful whether or not you have a good relationship with your father. In fact, in some ways they will be even more useful if you have a bad relationship, when coming to terms with your father would have to involve a reconciliation.

Second, in the most general sense the procedures are geared to accomplishing two essential ends: the de-idealization of your father and understanding his experience.

Finally—and this is crucial—as you will soon see, much of the work involved in making peace with your father is accomplished within yourself. This is why it's possible to come to terms with father even when he is unavailable.

There are two kinds of inner work you must do. The first is intellectual, the second emotional.

The activities in this section of the chapter are particularly useful for helping you become aware of your father's emotional and familial baggage and its impact on you. Keeping his burdens in mind should help you engage in constructive dialogue with him if that's on your personal agenda. A set of guidelines for such dialogues appears later in the chapter.

# Intellectual Inner Work

Intellectual inner work can help you get to know your father as a person and shed the paternal stereotypes you may have clung to until now (see Chapter 3). You need to get to know your father as a flawed human being, to deepen your understanding and appreciation of him as a person struggling in his own life to find meaning and achieve a sense of integrity. Speaking metaphorically, these techniques are designed to pull back the curtain to reveal the real Wizard of Oz—a mere mortal with lots of failings and limitations.

Three techniques, presented below, are especially helpful. They can be used singly or in combination. Although all three share some similarities, each makes it possible to gain specific insights not provided by the others.

## Technique 1: An Undistorted Look at Dad

The following inventory can help you correct your mistaken notions about your father and form a more accurate picture of him. You will be asked to respond to many questions about your father as a person. To use the inventory to its maximum advantage, follow these instructions:

- Make at least three copies of the blank inventory.

- Complete one copy of your own first. Base your answers on your own understanding and impressions. Answer each question as fully as you can. If you cannot answer a question, leave it blank.

- After you've completed your copy of the inventory, consult with someone who has been familiar with your father over a long period of time, and whose judgment, perceptions, and intelligence you trust. Some possibilities are a family elder, one of his lifelong friends, or a long-time co-worker or business associate. You may want to consult more than one such person, if they exist. If they are willing to complete a copy of the inventory, have them do so. If they would prefer just to talk, then arrange one or more meetings. (In the unlikely event that you can find no one who is able or willing to provide the kind of information you're looking for, you'll have no choice but to paint as complete a picture as you can, using the information that *is* available to you. This might include letters, diaries, even photographs.)

- If your father is available and capable of it, have him complete a copy of the inventory himself.

- After all your data have been collected, compare your impressions with the answers and insights provided by others (if, as noted, others have provided data). Combine everyone's answers to form as accurate a picture as you can.

- If possible, and if the material is not too devastating, discuss the results of your investigation with your father. Naturally, you will not serve your purposes by simply heaping abuse on him.

- Note that throughout the inventory questions are phrased with the assumption that your father is still alive. Reword the questions if he is not.

- Finally, wherever appropriate, distinguish between your father as he is now and as he was at an earlier time in your life. You may want to answer particular questions from both perspectives.

- Use extra paper if your answers require more room than the space provided. Add any other questions that would be of interest to you.

## *Inventory:*
## *An Undistorted Look at Dad*

1. What are my father's greatest strengths as a person? His greatest weaknesses?

   _____

   _____

2. What is his greatest source of pleasure in life? Has this changed over the years?

   _____

   _____

3. What is his greatest source of pain or disappointment? What's his greatest source of embarrassment? Have these changed?

   _____

   _____

4. Has my father been happy and successful in his career? His marriage? His social life? Has he always been? If not, why?

   _____

   _____

5. When I was growing up, how did my father's frustrations and disappointments affect his behavior toward me? My mother? My siblings? Others?

   _____

   _____

6. What are my father's greatest objective or measurable accomplishments? His greatest overt failures?

   _____

   _____

7. What pressures affected my father during my childhood, adolescence, and young adulthood? Did the pressures change over the years in degree or kind? How did these pressures affect him? What impact did this have on me?

   _____

8. When I was growing up, did my father have reason to be anxious about me? Did I have important physical or other problems that might have shaped his behavior toward me? How?

_____

_____

9. Did my father see me as capable of making my way in the world? Why or why not? Does his perspective make sense to me? Why or why not?

_____

_____

10. What is my father's fondest wish? His deepest secret? His most bitter memory? His most secret desire?

_____

_____

## Technique 2: The Father-Son Timeline

This technique is especially useful in helping you understand your father and follow the course of his life as he's experienced it. Besides compiling data about your father, you'll be able to construct a worksheet that allows you to trace the important events and influences that had an impact on your relationship from the time of your birth.

For the purposes of this activity, divide your father's life into two broad periods: the part of his life that preceded your birth, and the part that followed it.

For the period prior to your birth, you will have to do some research. To understand your father's life experience during that period, talk with him, his siblings, relatives, friends—anyone who knew him and his family during his childhood and young adulthood. Your mother, too, may be able to provide answers. See if you can gain access to diaries, letters, and photos, especially if there is no one whom you can consult in person.

Here are the sorts of questions to ask:

**What characterized my father's childhood and early life experience?**

*Parental relationship and history*

- What kind of relationship did my father's parents have? Were they happy together? Were there any serious problems in the relationship?

- How did his parents meet? Under what conditions were they married? Did my great-grandparents approve of the marriage?

*Family experience*

- Under what physical, emotional, and financial conditions did my father grow up?

- What kind of relationships did he have with his parents, especially his father?

- What major influences shaped his experience? His family's? For example, was his father financially successful? Was his father abusive? Alcoholic? Happy in his marriage, work, and social life? Did he have good health?

- To what degree was my father's early life experience shaped by physical or emotional illness? Infidelity? Separation? Divorce? Abandonment? Death? Family conflict? Physical deprivation?

*Temperament and development*

- What was my father like as a child? What about as an adolescent?

- What kind of person did my father become as he approached adulthood?

Recast these questions as the actual conditions of your father's life demand. Feel free to add questions as appropriate.

Then compile your answers. Depending on how organized and systematic you want to be, you might consider labeling a series of file folders with such headings as *Grandparents' marriage, Father's life as a preschooler, Father's life: 6-13 years old*. You can use the file folders for the data you accumulate.

One patient who used this technique wrote his answers on looseleaf paper, organized in a three-ring binder, using colored tabs to separate one block of questions from another. It was easy for him to add pages with more information as he gathered it.

For the period following your birth, divide your father's life into different eras, making logical divisions based on important events. These eras can range from several months to several years. Use smaller time increments during periods when many things were going on in his life, and larger ones during periods that seem to have been relatively quiet.

To construct your worksheet, make five vertical columns on a blank page. Label each column, from left to right, as follows: *Year/Timeframe, My Age, My Concerns, Father's Age, Father's Concerns*. Refer to the example below.

| Year/ Time- frame | My Age | My Concerns | Father's Age | Father's Concerns |
| --- | --- | --- | --- | --- |

Make at least ten photocopies of the blank form. Then, in the lefthand column, write the year, timeframe, or period on which you are focusing. In the second column, write your age range during the time you've selected (for instance, age 11-13). In the third column, briefly describe your concerns during that time. "Concerns" can mean anything from the issues you were grappling with to events that mattered to you (such as starting kindergarten or grade school), as well as worries or problems you had to deal with. In the fourth column, write your father's age or age range at that time. In the fifth column, list the events, issues, and concerns that affected him in his life during that period, whether they had to do with work or career, finances, his family of origin, his health, or whatever.

The timeline approach enables you to see immediately the concurrent concerns of you and your father. If the two of you were "out of phase"—if your otherwise caring and involved father was emotionally unavailable to you during a particular period of your youth—the timeline can help you find out why. It also enables you to see yourself from your father's perspective as you may never have done before.

Once again, in completing the timeline, it would be advisable to rely not only on your own perceptions and recollections, but also on data provided by others. If your father did not bring home his concerns and troubles, you could not know then what they were; nor can you know now. Therefore, speak with people who might have known then what was going on. Many of the same sources of information mentioned above can be consulted: a family elder, your mother, older siblings, other relatives, family friends, your father's co-workers, and so on.

If possible, have your father complete the timeline himself, recalling his own experience as your life unfolded.

The example that follows illustrates what your worksheet might look like.

### *Worksheet: Father-Son Timeline*

| Year/ Time-frame | My Age | My Concerns | Father's Age | Father's Concerns |
|---|---|---|---|---|
| 1944-1945 | 0-1 | Feeding and survival | 37 | Second child born. His other, a son, was 5 years old at the time. Concerns: (1) providing for the family (2) running his own manufacturing business (3) his health: |

his hearing and eyesight were poor, creating in him and Mom considerable apprehension about his ability to continue to provide for the family (4) his parents, whom he'd left behind in Spain 20 years earlier, were aging and needed his financial help (5) the USA was in the midst of WW II, although he was not draft-eligible for health reasons (6) the war provided many new business opportunities, but it also resulted in shortages of food, heating oil, and other necessities upon which our family relied

| 1945-1950 | 1-6 | Intimate tie with mother; entering the world; connecting with parents and brother; socializing with other tots; preparing for school | 38-43 | Family moved out of an apartment and bought a home. Older son began primary school. Concerns: (1) financial pressures of home ownership (2) business demands (3) ongoing health issues, his own, and his wife's (miscarriage, 1948) (5) his lack of formal education made it impossible for him to offer much help |

to his older son and
was a source of embar-
rassment to him

Go into as much detail as you want to; but don't get so involved in one period that you don't carry the timeline up to the present. You might begin by sketching in major events and themes, adding more detail if you want to later.

Once you've compiled and recorded the information on your father-son timeline, step back and study it. You may uncover correlations between your experience and the events in your father's life (or concerns that were felt at particular points in your life). For example, the death of one of his parents during your fourteenth year may account for his having behaved in a depressed and detached manner at the time. An extramarital affair that you found out about later may have shaped his way of dealing at a particular time with you, your mother, and your siblings.

As you've already seen, the timeline can be used retrospectively, to make sense of what has already occurred. But it can also be used prospectively. Suppose the information suggests that your father typically withdraws when he is under stress, causing you to feel rejected and anxious. The timeline can help you anticipate upcoming events that are likely to cause him stress (for example, retirement or problems with his physical health) and recognize in advance that they may result in his withdrawing again. By anticipating his reaction, you can prepare for it and perhaps change your unconstructive and previously automatic reactions.

Finally, the timeline may help you predict your own reactions to upcoming events in your life. Like many of my clients, you may find that the timeline helps you recognize your father's behavior in yourself. If you learn that you behave similarly to your father under parallel circumstances, then you can predict your reactions and exert more control over them. Let's suppose you have a son of your own. Rather than following in your father's footsteps as your boy reaches adolescence, you may elect to break the pattern, substituting more involvement for less, and open communication for an authoritarian style of communication.

## Technique 3: The Family Geneological Portrait

The third technique provides a way to create a comprehensive family tree that shows the biological, legal, and emotional connections among your family members; significant events and their causes in the life of the family (including marriages, divorces, births, and deaths; personal histories (including work and school experiences, educational attainment, and health information); and other data—for example, if one child was favored by one parent or the other—that can help you understand the context from which family members and their behavior have emerged.

Any portrait that includes so much detail must necessarily be time-consuming to create. It must also be physically constructed on a large enough scale to provide room for all the material. Like the two techniques described so far, this one will require that you consult with family elders and others who are in a position to fill in missing information. I suggest that you proceed as follows:

- Gather necessary information and as much detail as possible. Wherever possible, include dates for significant family events and changes; at the very least, provide as precise a timeframe as you can.

- Create your geneological portrait in small pieces at first, on separate sheets of paper. Each piece should focus on a particular individual or subunit within the family.

- Later, begin linking together the mini-portraits you've created.

- Plan to do a few drafts on large pieces of inexpensive paper—colored marking pens work well. Some of my clients have used the back of large rolls of gift-wrapping paper or rolls of butcher paper. You can also buy rolls of inexpensive paper in crafts or art-supply stores (continuous-form computer paper works well, too).

- When you've worked out the kinks, you can transfer your completed portrait to a piece of poster board or some other sturdy surface.

A well-crafted family portrait can not only help you deepen your understanding of your father and your relationship with him, it can also shed light on your own experience, thinking, and behavior. For example, in gathering information for your family portrait, you may learn that, within your family, firstborn males have tended to have more conflicted relationships with their fathers than later-born sons. This may help you understand why your father's relationship with an older brother is so much more conflicted than his relationship with you.

The portrait can also help predict certain events and crises. For instance, one man's family map showed that in the generation preceding his, three out of four men underwent major emotional crises in their late thirties. One divorced his wife after becoming involved with a woman many years his junior. A second impulsively left a successful career to pursue a fantasy of becoming a gentleman farmer. And a third was hospitalized for a depression that reached clinical proportions. The man who prepared this family tree was able to predict that he might also be vulnerable to such emotional crises unless he took steps to address the unresolved problems in his life.

Finally, a family portrait can reveal important patterns, such as substance abuse on one or both sides of the family, troubled marital relationships among the children of parents who were unhappy together, or a tendency on the part of sons to remain emotionally wedded to Mother well into their adulthood. All this information can elucidate your feelings and experiences while forewarning you of problems that might occur if you don't seek help or initiate change.

There are 11 conventional symbols used in the construction of family portraits. Getting into the habit of using them will save you time and eliminate confusion. They appear below. Consult these symbols as you begin sketching the portrait, and refer to them as often as you need to. If unique circumstances require that you invent additional symbols, do so; create a key legend so you will always know what each symbol means.

| Symbol | Meaning | Comments |
|---|---|---|
| ☐ | Male | Names and dates of birth and death are placed as close as possible to the symbol for the individual involved. |
| ◯ | Female | |
| 31 | Present age | A number inside a square or a circle indicates the person's age at the present time. |
| ⊗ | Dead | A person's age at death is noted by putting it in parentheses after the date of death is noted. The cause of death, if known, should be put in the same parentheses. |
| _____ | Married to | Children are listed below a horizontal line that indicates a marriage. They are recorded from left to right, in the order of their birth. (The oldest child appears on the far left, the youngest on the far right.) The generations are listed from top |

to bottom, with the oldest
generation at the top of the
portrait and the youngest at the
bottom.

————/———— Separated from

————//———— Divorced from

— — — — —  Distant from    This and the following three
symbols are modifiers, describ-
ing the kind of relationship two
people have. Write these symbols in a different color in
order to avoid confusion.

——————  Calm and
connected

========  Emotionally
intense

〰〰〰  Conflicted

These symbols are a sort of shorthand. But not every fact
about a person can be recorded in symbolic form. You will need
to write in certain facts, such as a person's career, educational
attainment, and personal traits (for example, "alcoholic").

On page 159 is an example of a family portrait. Study it
for a while until you see the various kinds of information it contains. Then begin gathering information for your own geneological chart.

# Emotional Inner Work

The second kind of inner work you must do to make peace with
your father is emotional. This work enables you to acknowledge
and resolve feelings, especially negative ones, that can make it
impossible to close the door on your relationship with your fa-

ther, improve a marginal relationship, or reestablish one that has been severely strained.

The four techniques described here, used singly or in various combinations, can help you come to grips with your relationship with your father. If your father is available, the techniques can help you identify issues you need to discuss with him, pointing the way to hitherto unspoken topics and feelings that demand talking out. Whether or not your father is alive, you should use these techniques on your own, without your father's participation. If he is around, you may choose to share some of the results of your emotional work with him. But this is by no means a necessity.

Should you have the opportunity and the desire to engage in a dialogue with your father, you'll be given guidance later in this chapter about how to do it. For now, bear one crucial point in mind: if you have successfully used the techniques described here, your dialogue with him will be uncontaminated by a need to shame, blame, or humiliate him.

## Letter Writing

The first technique involves writing a series of letters to your father in which you talk about past experiences. These letters are not for mailing, but for your benefit alone. By sorting out feelings and taking the time to put your thoughts and sentiments into words, you give form to emotions and wishes that may never have made their way into your conscious mind.

Many people find that one or two letters, written in the dead heat of emotion, don't offer much help. Instead, you should plan to write several letters at various times and when you are in different states of mind. Some letters can be written when thoughts or recollections leave you feeling grateful to your father. Others can be written when you're feeling disappointed in him, or angry. No matter how many letters you write, or how long it takes you to write them all, the entire series should capture the range of feelings you have toward him.

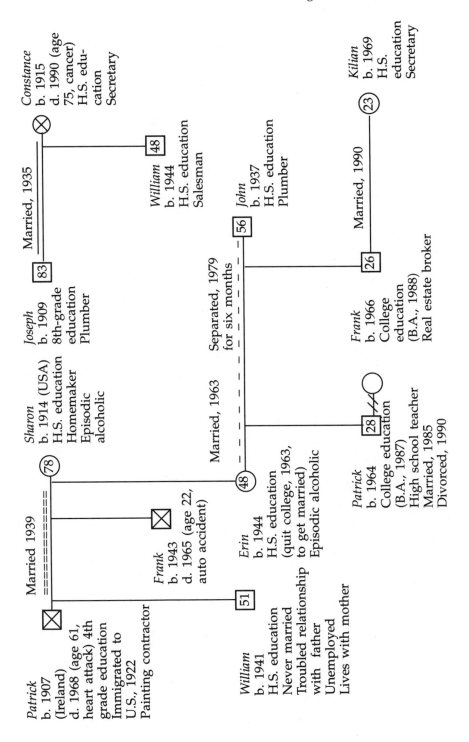

Some men have asked me whether their letters should contain anything in particular. There are no hard-and-fast rules with respect to content. You can use your letters to recall your unfulfilled wishes and disappointments. You can write about experiences you shared with your dad—those that you treasure most or those that were most painful. You can review the satisfactions you knew in your relationship with him as a child and an adolescent. You can talk about current or recent experiences and your hopes for the future.

When dealing with past experiences, there are two guiding principles that ought to govern your writing. First, describe each experience in as much detail as possible. Don't say simply, "I was upset when you didn't come to my high school graduation ceremony." Instead, describe the ceremony, the setting, the people who did attend, and so on. The idea here is to conjure up as many memories as possible (including sense memories such as the temperature of the hall, the sights and smells, and the kind of music played by the band) so that you can virtually relive the experience. Then talk about the impact your father's absence had on you. Make a real effort to describe your experience and your feelings in detail. Imagine your father reading the letter, and try hard to express yourself so that he will completely understand how you reacted and why.

The other principle to follow is this: whenever possible, close your letter with a paragraph or two that brings the matter to a close. State what it was you wanted from your father. Tell what you would want from him if he were around now. If you describe a hurt he inflicted, forgive him if you can; if you can't say so, then express the net effect of his behavior on you. The point here is to not leave matters unresolved, but rather to achieve a sense of closure.

Some men find that they need to write more than one letter focusing on one specific event or experience. If you have suffered a severe trauma, for example, you may need to write several letters. One man I worked with was only nine years old when his father was stabbed to death in a bar brawl. He wrote four different letters to his father. One letter expressed his rage at his father for having abandoned the family. Another expressed his tremendous feelings of loss; in it he told how much he had missed his father at virtually every important point in his life, most especially when his own son was born. A third coldly informed his father, with some resentment, of what it was like to have been cast in the role of a man of the family at such an early age. A fourth simply updated his father on what had happened to his son, daughter, and wife in his absence.

To gain the maximum benefit from the letters you write, you will almost certainly need to talk with someone about what you've written and how the experience affected you. A professional therapist, a professionally led men's group, or even a well-run self-help group can afford you this opportunity.

## Creating Art

Another technique is to create a work of art designed to capture how you feel or summarize how it's been for you as your father's son. This creation can be real or imaginary. Make a mask or set of masks, compose a song, paint a painting, write a story or poem, create a sculpture or collage. If you're not someone who normally creates art, it may help you to take a class that will at least provide materials, such as paints or clay. The goal isn't to produce great art, but rather to find an alternative format for your emotions, one that may make them easier to express. So find your medium—whether fingerpaints, musical notes, words, or charcoal—and let yourself give free rein to your feelings. Try to create art with the same lack of inhibition as a young child.

If for any reason you prefer not to create an actual work, try this. In your mind's eye, create a sculpture that depicts the relationship between you and your father. Use any materials you wish: stone, cloth, wood, etc. Your imaginary work can include more than one medium—for example, a stone father and a cloth son. Your sculpture can be as small or as large as you like. The relative size of the figures is also a matter of your own choosing (relative size can reflect the psychological relationship between the two of you). The figures in your sculpture can be static, caught in the midst of a shared moment. Or they can be dynamic, able to twist or move separately or in unison. The possibilities are endless. Just remember that the sculpture you create should attempt to capture the most important truths about your relationship with your father, and serve as a way for you to express your feelings about it.

## Writing Your Father's Obituary

Writing your father's obituary, whether or not he is actually dead, can also help you sort out your feelings and come to grips with him. The obituary can be as creative and unconventional as you like, but it should include specific information about his fathering. The point of the exercise is to delineate his successes and failures as the father of all his children, and especially you. (Remember—the obituary doesn't have to be balanced or traditional in tone or format; it should, instead, reflect your personal recollections and feelings.) Here's an example that begins conventionally, then changes in tone.

> Tamas Howard, 80, of 33 Village Street, Phillipstown, Iowa, died Friday at the Woodland Convalescent Center after a brief illness. Born in Elmira, New York, December 6, 1913, he as the son of the late Tamas and Helga Howard. After graduating from high school, Mr. Howard worked as an auto body repairman until his retirement in 1978. At the time of his death he operated T. Howard and Son Auto Body on Green Street, Phillipstown. He is survived by two sons, John of Phillipstown and Gregory of New York City; a brother, Andrei, of Atlanta, Georgia; and three grandchildren.
>
> Mr. Howard was a hard-working man and a good provider, but his performance as a father was

uneven. He was particularly fond of his elder son, John, and he treated his two boys very differently. He and John shared many interests, automobile repair and metalworking chief among them. Eventually, John became a partner in the family auto body repair business.

For his part, Gregory felt for most of his life like an "also ran." Different from his father and his elder brother, Gregory is still uncertain whether his lack of interest in auto body repair was the cause of his having drifted emotionally from his father and brother, or the result of it. Nor does he know whether his cool relationship with John is the result of their different temperaments and talents or the consequence of their having been treated so differently by Tamas.

Interestingly, Tamas was also the older of two sons, and was favored by his father at the expense of Andrei. Perhaps this helps explain his inability to avoid playing favorites in his own family.

Gregory's fondest memories of his father are from his earliest years. He has memories of his father playing with him in the evening after dinner while Mrs. Howard was shopping with friends. He recalls taking his broken toys to his father for repair, watching him build a scooter out of an old crate, a plank of wood, and an old roller skate, and marveling at his ability to fix everything from leaky faucets to television sets. He remembers all this fondly, but wishes he'd been allowed to participate at least some of the time rather than just watch.

His least pleasant memories center around his father's conspicuous lack of interest in Gregory's accomplishments as a painter. More than once, he remembers proudly showing his paintings to his father, only to have them acknowledged with hollow-sounding praise. He remembers thinking, "It'd be better to say nothing than to mouth such empty words." In retrospect, it may be that his father genuinely couldn't appreciate the paintings. But, somehow, Gregory is left with the feeling that they'd have gotten a more enthusiastic reception had John created them.

All in all, Gregory is grateful for all his father did for him, but he regrets that the two of them could not get closer before Tamas died. He can't help feeling this was his father's choice, not his.

This exercise can be carried further still. After you have written your father's obituary, imagine that you died at your current age. Write your own obituary. Stress points of similarity and difference between you and your father. Describe in specific terms how your father's relationship with you shaped you as a person and, if you are a father, influenced your behavior toward your children.

You will probably not be able to complete this activity in one sitting. Some of my patients have found that it takes several sittings, and many drafts, to say precisely what needs to be said. But almost all have found that the work provided a significant payoff in terms of self-awareness and an appreciation of their father's experience.

Writing dual obituaries for yourself and your father can also help you sort out your feelings and come to grips with him. The obituaries can be as creative and unconventional as you like. Stress points of similarity and difference. Don't fail to discuss both the good and the bad in your shared experiences.

## Staging an Imagined Dialogue

The final technique may well be the most powerful, although many men find that the guidance of a trained therapist is necessary for the technique to be maximally effective. It involves engaging in imaginary conversations with your father. The goal is not to rehearse for any upcoming conversation in real life, but simply to vent your feelings. Tell your dad what you've always wanted to say but never could. Let him know what you need from him (you can conduct your part of the dialogue playing yourself as a child if you wish). Talk about special events in your past, your reactions to his behavior. If he let you down in significant ways, tell him about it. Talk about anything you'd like, including your family's experiences as well as your individual ones. Don't be afraid to be angry, to show your hurt.

These conversations shouldn't be one-sided. Play your father, too. Speak back to yourself as he might. If it would be characteristic of him to make excuses when confronted, make them. Then respond as yourself to his excuses. If he would be likely to respond by expressing his anger in a sullen silence, behave as he might. Then respond to his silence—tell him how it's always made you feel for him to behave that way. Goad him into a response. Capture the give-and-take of an actual conversation, giving both sides an opportunity to fully express feelings and react to each other as they might in an actual conversation.

Use two chairs for this exercise. Sitting in one, speak as yourself, addressing your father in the empty chair. Sitting in the other, speak as your father. As you move from one chair to the other, assume the posture, facial expressions, and other characteristics of each of the two people talking.

Most people find this technique forced and artifical at first; after you get going, though, it may come to feel quite natural. You may be surprised at the power of this technique to bring forth buried feelings. Role-playing your father can also help you understand his point of view—even if you ultimately find his actions unforgivable.

## Dos and Don'ts

You need to read this section of the chapter only if you plan to have one or more actual conversations with your father based on the work you've done here. (I strongly recommend more than one.) There are specific suggestions, based on the experiences of many men with whom I've worked, about what to expect, how to handle yourself, and what to avoid doing during a confrontation with your dad.

I've chosen a very prescriptive approach (do this, don't do that) to make my points as directly as possible. Like all such prescriptions, these should be interpreted in light of individual circumstances: the kind of relationship you have (or don't have) with your father, your health and his, and your individual goals.

## Dos

Be clear in your own mind about what your goals are. Know what you want from your father now, in the present time (you're not going to be able to change what has already happened). Have a clear sense of what would constitute a successful outcome of your meeting.

Be certain that an actual face-to-face conversation would be worthwhile and productive. Some goals are better achieved in other ways.

Take responsibility for initiating contact. Since it's you who need to clear the air and unearth old issues, the burden falls on you to arrange a meeting. This can be very difficult if your father has not been part of your life for a long time. It may require repeated contacts and negotiations about time and place. The task may be difficult and aggravating.

Expect your father to be surprised, confused, bewildered, and perhaps even rejecting in reaction to your request. In my experience, few fathers gracefully accept a son's efforts to break through a wall of silence that may span decades. If you are put off by his shock or rejection, one more hurdle will be created in your efforts to reach your father. Anticipate his reactions so that you're not thrown by them.

Prepare him for your upcoming conversation. It's inadvisable to surprise him with your need for a deeper, more meaningful relationship, or to force a conversation that he's not prepared for. One of the worst times to attempt meaningful dialogue is at a family gathering. Even though a family occasion may seem like a convenient time to proceed, you should pick another time when you and your father can be alone.

You can prepare your father in several ways. Here are two of the most direct. Write him one or more letters in which you let him know your intentions. Provide background and insight into your motivations. For example, if your desire for a dialogue stems from your reading about fathers and sons, or from your experiences in psychotherapy, tell him. (You might even recommend that he read this book.) Help him understand why you want to talk.

Another way is to initiate one or more phone conversations. If it's been your custom to speak with your mother when you call your parents, ask to speak with your father. Do this a few times. Slowly broach the subject of your wanting to address some father-son issues; when your intentions are clear, and your father understands what you want to do and why, arrange for a face-to-face conversation.

In any actual conversation, go slowly. Avoid rushing headlong into hot issues that are likely to abort dialogue before it's actually begun. Give careful thought to the order in which your concerns and questions can be most productively raised.

Consider planning joint activities that can provide a natural framework for conversation. Some possibilities: Take a drive together. Play a round of golf. Visit a place you both enjoy where conversation will be possible (a museum, a restaurant, a bar, a state park, the beach). Go back to your old neighborhood, or drive by the house or apartment in which you grew up.

Tactfully share some or all of the results of the intellectual preparation you've done—your inventory, the father-son timeline, and the geneological portrait. Tell your dad what you've learned about him and his life, and ask for corroboration. Invite him to make additions to the inventory, the timeline, and the family tree. Joint activities like these provide numerous opportunities for meaningful talk.

### Don'ts

Don't shame or humiliate your father. That will only drive him away. As noted earlier, any need to shame him is a clear indication that you have failed to complete the intellectual and emotional inner work discussed in the previous section of the chapter. Your goals ought to be to understand your father, deepen your appreciation of his life experience, and see more clearly than you have before the basis for his behavior.

If this book has taught you nothing else, it should have taught you that your father likely carried into his adulthood his own share of pain and loss. Don't add to it by using your conversations with him as an opportunity to inflict still more agony.

Don't compare your father with other fathers, or yourself with other sons. Comparisons are almost always experienced as threatening, a way of saying: "You don't quite measure up," or "You're not good enough the way you are." By avoiding comparisons, you'll reduce defensiveness and make meaningful dialogue more possible.

Don't try to get your father to apologize for his faults or for his having failed you as a father. The point is to express your feelings rather than to manipulate his. If you can get him to acknowledge your feelings, consider yourself to be doing well. Your dad is not going to change because you've had the courage to speak with him honestly. The past won't change either. What you *can* hope to change is your future by getting some old, bad feelings off your chest.

## To Summarize

In this chapter you've learned why it's so essential to make peace with your father. You've seen the emotional obstacles that stand in your way, and learned about the inner work—both intellectual and emotional—that's necessary to come to grips with your dad, whether he is dead or alive, present or absent from your life.

# Recommended Reading

Emerson, G. (1985) *Some American Men*. New York: Simon and Schuster.

Fanning, P., and M. McKay. (1993) *Being a Man: A Guide to the New Masculinity*. Oakland, CA: New Harbinger Publications, Inc.

Forward, S. (1989) *Toxic Parents: Overcoming the Hurtful Legacy and Reclaiming Your Life*. New York: Bantam Books.

Janov, A. (1972) *The Primal Scream*. New York: Dell Publishing Co.

Lerner, H. G. (1985) *The Dance of Anger: A Woman's Guide to Changing the Patterns of Intimate Relationships*. New York: Harper and Row.

Mayer, N. (1978) *The Male Mid-Life Crisis: Fresh Starts After 40*. New York: New American Library.

Petras. J. W., ed. (1975) *Sex: Male, Gender: Masculine*. Port Washington, New York: Alfred Publishing Co.

Vogt, G. M., and S. T. Stirridge. (1991) *Like Son, Like Father*. New York: Plenum Press.

# 8

# Overcoming Barriers to Communication

Some of the barriers that impede communication between fathers and sons are obvious: a father who does not listen or is harshly critical of his son at every opportunity; a son whose sarcastic and disrespectful manner puts his father off. Such behaviors can erect enormous barriers, many of them seemingly insurmountable.

Other barriers are less obvious. In fact, the patterns that constitute the most significant impediments to communication between fathers and sons are typically unconscious and automatic: they feel natural and seem to be unavoidable. They are the product of the cultural conditioning males receive, and may escape the awareness of fathers and sons altogether, not seeming to require any attention. Of the two types of barriers, the less obvious ones are the more pernicious. They are the focus of this chapter.

# Barriers to Communication Between Males

## Cultural Conditioning and Barriers to Communication

Every culture empowers and impedes. Being raised in a culture provides you with a particular view of your physical, interpersonal and psychological environment, as well as with the tools and skills essential to survival. At the same time, members of a culture learn to experience life within quite specific limits. The world-view that enables you to fit comfortably within your native culture simultaneously excludes you from others. It also makes it impossible for you to see reality as people raised in other cultures do.

For example, if you're the product of Western European culture, you likely have one view of man's place on earth and his relationship to his environment. The perspectives of people raised in other cultures—Native Americans and Asians, for example—may seem alien. As a subscriber to the Judeo-Christian tradition, you may not be able to share the wisdom, inner life, or experienced benefits of these "alien" peoples. Yet these other cultural systems are also viable resources for satisfying ways of life. Chinese medicine works—for those who accept its premises. Even the incantations of medicine men work—for those who share the world-view from which the shamanistic tradition springs. (If you're intrigued by this idea, you'll enjoy the suggested readings listed at the end of this chapter, most especially those of Edward T. Hall and E. Fuller Torrey.)

Like all members of our culture, males born into it are both empowered and impeded. They learn essential skills and habits of mind that identify them as males and make it possible for them to function completely. But they also learn many ways of being that are limiting and even tragically debilitating.

Among the most unfortunate consequences of growing up male in this culture is a style of communicating that has a distinctly adverse effect on relationships, especially the relationship between fathers and sons. The following questionnaire can help you get a sense of how cultural conditioning has affected your behavior in relationships.

## Communication Conditioning: A Questionnaire

|  | Yes | No |
|---|---|---|
| 1. I am comfortable and even enjoy talking openly with other men about personal worries, relationship concerns, and other private matters. |  |  |
| 2. In my opinion, communication with men is a way of getting close to them and cementing relationships. |  |  |
| 3. A satisfying conversation with a male friend doesn't need to accomplish any particular purpose, nor must it be focused on a task or some factual subject matter; it only needs to give each guy an opportunity to share feelings and get closer to one another. |  |  |
| 4. When I'm upset, I find it easy and comfortable to ask for and receive spoken support and compassion from male friends. |  |  |
| 5. When I talk about personal problems and concerns with other men, I don't expect help in finding solutions; rather, I want to feel understood and to know that my friends are empathic. My goal is to achieve a sense of connection, understanding, and empathy. |  |  |

|  | Yes | No |
|---|---|---|
| 6. I wouldn't want to drive others away by appearing strong and indifferent to their attention when I am hurting and in need of sympathy or understanding. |  |  |
| 7. My male friends and I can cry together if we are moved by some sad event, acute distress, or extreme frustration. |  |  |
| 8. I am comfortable displaying to male friends traits like dependency, fearfulness, and emotional neediness; I wouldn't feel like a wimp displaying any of those traits. |  |  |
| 9. I can openly and directly talk about my feelings of affection and regard for a male friend without feeling awkward or uncomfortable. |  |  |
| 10. I can comfortably talk to other men about domestic subjects like cooking, child-rearing, and homemaking. |  |  |

Did you answer most questions "yes" or "no"? Your answers were likely determined by your gender. Unless you're a very unusual man indeed, you probably answered very few of the questions affirmatively. Men have it beaten into them in our culture that there are certain things they simply cannot say and do if they are to be taken seriously as males. Among these taboos are talking openly about your feelings to other men, crying, and directly asking male friends or relatives for emotional support.

This cultural conditioning adversely affects the relationship between fathers and sons. It does so both directly and indirectly.

## Communication Conditioning and
## Father-Son Relationships

*Cultural conditioning emphasizes hierarchy over intimacy in relationships between men.* According to socio-linguist Deborah Tannen, this is the single most important feature of male communication conditioning; it also engenders almost all other impediments to communication between men.

It's no accident that almost all little boys' games are competitive. Confrontation, challenges, even pushing and shoving are unavoidable. (The game "king of the mountain" comes to mind as a quintessential boys' game.) In male games, winning and leading are highly desirable. Being able to give orders is clearly preferable to being in a position of taking them.

This kind of play teaches the players to be conscious of hierarchy, preparing them for an inherently competitive world of men. If he is to succeed as a male, a boy must learn to achieve and compete, to be able to become the "king of the mountain" and maintain his position.

In the course of playing gender-specific games, boys learn two crucial lessons about communication. First, they learn that the primary purpose of talk is to establish and maintain a dominant position in the social hierarchy. Boys are more likely than girls to claim authority over playmates by giving orders and directives. This behavior carries over into adulthood.

Second, boys learn that a key purpose of verbal interaction is to impart information. "Good talk" should be impersonal, fact-based, and task-focused.

By contrast, girls' games teach cooperation and intimacy. (Some boys' games, especially team sports, teach cooperation. However, working together is simply a way of defeating another group of boys who are cooperating for the same reason: to defeat your team.) Girls learn to share feelings and talk openly about their concerns and problems. If you observe a play-group of girls, you'll see that being on top in the social hierarchy is

must less important than being able to listen to others and respond in a caring way. Consequently, girls achieve status in a
group by being good friends to others rather than by claiming
the right to give orders.

Conditioning for hierarchy affects the relationship between
fathers and sons in two ways. First, it creates in men a style of
communicating that feels very natural but may be experienced
by little boys as enigmatic and remote. Long before a man has
become a father, he's learned to reveal very little of his inner
life. He knows that to discuss his problems, concerns, and feelings is considered a sign of weakness by other males. As a father,
he knows (or rather, fears) that doing so would be considered
a sign of weakness by his son.

It's not surprising that sons rarely get to know their father
as a person—emotional, vulnerable, and human. Instead, they
see him as a figure and a force—a large, almost cartoonlike character who is apparently without an inner life. The existence of
the father stereotypes discussed in Chapter 3 (for example, "The
Invulnerable Father") suggests that the typical father behaves in
ways that dehumanize him, making him difficult to connect with
emotionally.

The fact that male communication conditioning emphasizes hierarchy over intimacy places father in a double bind
when it comes to nurturing his son. On the one hand, he must
help in the only way he knows how, namely by assuming a position of superiority and giving advice, instruction, and criticism.
Lecturing his son, seeking compliance and submission—all this
is safe and familiar, whereas talking about emotions feels unfamiliar and dangerous.

When a father does nurture in this way, his efforts almost
always create confusion and resentment. The son becomes confused: when a father says he wants to "have a talk," he rarely
means that he wants to have a give-and-take conversation. A
lecture is usually in the offing.

The son becomes resentful almost immediately. He's sensitive to being placed in a one-down position by virtue of being

the recipient of advice and criticism. (Boys rarely take kindly to behavior that threatens their status.)

The son reacts like any male who's been conditioned to rebuff unilateral claims to a position of superiority: he does his best to resist. He may interrupt in an attempt to sidetrack his father. He may convey nonacceptance of the status-threatening message by looking away, pretending not to listen to a word. Father perceives this behavior as disrespectful. In response, he becomes annoyed: "Look at me when I'm talking to you!" he commands. He thus exercises his authority and power to make the son comply. This is perceived as hostile by the son and thus evokes an equally hostile response. The situation goes downhill from there.

What began as a well-intended effort on father's part to fulfill his role as a caring parent ends in a disagreement and perhaps even worse. Howard Fast's 1962 novel, *April Morn*, opens with a poignant scene describing the interaction between a father and son. There and elsewhere in the book, Fast portrays the hurt, anger, and disillusionment experienced by 15-year-old Adam Cooper in response to his father's efforts to fulfill his paternal responsibility.)

Yet everything I've just said represents only one part of a father's double bind. The other is this: if he does nothing to guide his son—if he fails to help by setting his son straight, offering advice and criticism—he is considered to be uncaring and irresponsible. He may be accused of leaving the job of child-rearing to his wife or others.

Thus a crucial element in father's protective and nurturing role is inherently problematical. His well-intentioned behaviors, regardless of the direction they take, are bound to evoke confusion, animosity, and resentment—and probably all three.

The following table shows the most common psychological positions taken by a critic and a recipient of criticism (both males) in a situation when criticism or advice is offered. It also points out the likely response of the recipient (this response may or may not be openly revealed).

## Critic-Recipient Positions

**Role of Critic/Advisor:** Helpful, an information-giver

**Example:** A mentor explaining company policy to a new employee

**Position of Recipient:** Slightly one-down

**Recipient's Likely Response:** "I'll listen, but only so long as my status isn't threatened."

•

**Role of Critic/Advisor:** Helpful, an advisor whose help has been sought out

**Example:** A mentor giving asked-for advice (for example, responding to his charge's request for advice about a career move)

**Position of Recipient:** Moderately one-down

**Recipient's Likely Response:** "I'll listen since I've put myself down by asking for help, but only so long as I'm not demeaned."

•

**Role of Critic/Advisor:** Helpful, an advisor whose help has not been sought out.

**Example:** A father giving unwanted advice to his son, telling him what he should do about a problem at school or work

**Position of Recipient:** Significantly one-down

**Recipient's Likely Response:** "I resent your putting me down and questioning my independence and judgment!"

•

**Role of Critic/Advisor:** Scolder, judge

**Example:** A father bawling out a son

**Position of Recipient:** Extremely one-down

**Recipient's Likely Response:** "Oh shut up! Who are you to judge me and tell me what to do?"

*Cultural conditioning fails to prepare men to ask for or receive nurturing from others, especially other males.*  As a result of their hierarchy conditioning, men are uncomfortable being vulnerable and admitting their need for nurturing. To do so would be to sacrifice their status in a group. They are equally unprepared to nurture—in the sense of giving emotional help—directly, even when asked. To do so would be to seize a higher-status position, something men learn not to do when dealing with people they care about—especially men.

Few men can comfortably ask for emotional support from even their closest female relatives or friends. Even fewer can turn to other men when they are in need. Perhaps that is why the caseload of the typical psychotherapist has long been and continues to be predominantly female. Few men, indeed, can admit to having emotional problems or even to being in emotional distress. Such a self-definition implies that one is "weak."

The typical male, when beset by worries and concerns, withdraws into himself. He rarely shares his concerns directly. If another—a caring partner, for example—attempts to draw him out, he typically drives the person away lest he reveal his vulnerability and appear weak. The more in need of sympathy he is, the more likely is he to drive caregivers away.

Often men are equally incapable of providing emotional support, especially when the person needing support is a man. Early in their lives, boys learn to be solution-centered in their talk with other males. If you're fortunate enough to witness a conversation among adolescent males discussing problems—perhaps girlfriend difficulties—listen to what they say. The boy with the problem won't really ask for help; he will likely disguise his request with a joke or a narrative. The boy turned to for help will almost always discount and minimize the feelings of the person who's suffering with remarks that convey these meanings: "Yeah, women are like that," and "You'll get over it." To express sympathy directly would be to seize a higher place in the social hierarchy. (In men's groups, those who are in a position to console are considered superior to those who need consoling.) It's ironic but logical, therefore, that boys and men tend to react to another male who needs sympathy by minimizing that person's problem and discounting his feelings.

By contrast, girls learn early on to talk about their problems. Their intent is not so much to solve them as to achieve connection, understanding, and intimacy. Since they aren't trained as men are, they can ask for and provide comfort and support without jeopardizing their standing in a group. In fact, they are rewarded with higher status when they are most open in intimate relationships.

The fact that men are not prepared to ask for or give nurturing adversely affects father-son communication in a few ways. First, father is not seen as a reliable source of tenderness, love, or nurturing. Because he isn't viewed as someone who can meet his son's emotional needs, his offspring turns elsewhere, often with unspoken and ill-defined resentment at father for not "being there" or supporting him emotionally. Mother, by contrast, at least understands and is capable of responding to his feelings empathically.

Second, father feels shut out of his son's emotional life. When his boy has turned to him in the past, the youngster has been rebuffed by his father's ineptitude in emotional matters. The father doesn't interpret those past events as his son does, and so fails to connect them with the boy's tendency to keep his distance. The father wishes that his son would come to him with his worries and concerns; he feels he's denied the chance to help. Realizing that he's giving his son all he's capable of giving emotionally, the father often winds up unconsciously resenting the son for excluding him.

Finally, because of their lack of preparation in asking for and accepting nurturing, sons and fathers have a hard time together when either is in pain. They are like two blind men in a picture gallery—anxious to help each other, but equally incapable of seeing or describing the paintings.

*Males are conditioned to show their love not in words but symbolically, through their behavior.* To a man, affection is shown in actions, not in what he says. Boys learn from the time they are very young that it's risky to talk about tender feelings for another male, since doing so can subject them to ridicule and loss of status in their group. It's far safer to show they care by doing kind things but in ways that are not obvious. (Openly expressing affection for another man is very likely to cause a man, especially a young one, to be pegged as a homosexual in a group of males.)

Except during his son's earliest years, a father expresses affection only in obscure and indirect ways. Cultural conditioning gives him very few options with regard to showing his love and concern. He must operate within the constraints imposed by the traditional male role—to protect and provide. Thus a father who tunes up his son's car is expressing love as certainly as a mother who hugs her son and tells him that she loves him—although this may not be altogether apparent to the son.

This conditioning adversely affects father-son communication, causing misunderstanding and missed messages. A son must have a keen mind to recognize when father is showing love, since his ways of doing so are often so convoluted and indirect. The boy can mistakenly feel that he is being criticized—for example, when Dad tunes up the car, it may be interpreted as an unspoken criticism of the son for failing to maintain the vehicle. Under the circumstances, it's understandable (but not to the father) that the son would react with annoyance rather than gratitude. The son may feel unloved and emotionally abandoned when, in fact, his father is expressing his love as best and directly as he can.

As a result of such misinterpretations, a father may feel unappreciated, angry, and resentful: "Not only doesn't my son appreciate my act of love," he might say to himself, "but he's actually annoyed with me! Of all the nerve!"

## Cultural Conditioning Has an Indirect
## Negative Impact on Father-Son Relationships

*Fathers and sons find it easier to be angry with one another than to be tender.* As you've seen, fathers and sons often feel misunderstood, unloved, and unappreciated. This provides a ready fund of anger and resentment on which to draw.

Add to this another fact: expressing anger and hostility is less risky to a man's masculinity than expressing caring and affection. Being tender may mark a man as a sissy or a wimp.

*In many families, mother takes on the role of the emotional switchboard in the family.* Because a father is not trained to deal directly with emotions, he relinquishes to his wife the role of emotions manager for the family. She becomes the interpreter and communicator of everyone else's feelings. It's often the case that fathers and sons don't talk directly about the things that matter most to them: they communicate instead through the mother.

A mother may speak to her husband on behalf of her son, and vice versa: "Your father loves you very much," she'll assure her son after he's complained about father's indifference or insensitivity to his needs. "That's just his way." And to her husband she'll say, "Gerald really needs to know you love him. He thinks you have no interest in him."

The role of emotional switchboard is familiar to many mothers. For better or worse, it's one they're trained for and that may even feel natural to them. Moreover, it provides them with a way to meet some of their emotional needs by being close to their son. Unfortunately, it simultaneously widens the gap between father and son.

*A father's ability to control his emotions causes serious problems in two specific situations.* A father can go on for months and years in apparently complete control of his emotions. When under duress, however, his emotions can break through to the surface in a way that can be terrifying to the son.

One man told me that he remembered his father as invariably calm and self-possessed. But when the young man reached adolescence and significant emotional pressures began to build in the family, the father seemed to be transformed. This normally even-tempered man exploded in fits of rage that were as startling as they were intense. Fathers tend to express their love and approval around issues of accomplishment, rather than spontaneously and for no particular reason, as a mother might. Father's love may feel more conditional to the son than his mother's affection, which is not performance-based. So when a normally unemotional father shows anger, his son may fear a total withdrawal of love, whereas a mother can be angry without seeming to hate her son. Her love, however much it may be put in abeyance, never seems entirely lost.

# Overcoming Communication Barriers

In this section of the chapter you'll learn three key techniques that can help improve communication between you and your father. The first and most crucial is *initiating affective communication* (no, I don't mean *effective*, although this is also part of the concept). The second techniques involves *learning to give and receive criticism constructively*. The final tool is what I call *reframing*.

## Initiate Affective Communication

To communicate well with your father and other males, it's necessary to de-condition yourself: to acquire new habits, including new ways of thinking about communication. From this point forward, I'll speak only about communicating with your father; however, all of my recommendations can enrich your relationships with others, including your own son.)

Contrary to what you learned as a boy, communication serves a variety of crucial purposes; its primary function is not always to establish and maintain your position in a social hierarchy. "Good talk" need not be fact-based, impersonal, or task-focused. Among the key functions of communication is to build rapport between people, to create empathy and strengthen interpersonal ties.

### Share Yourself

By "initiating affective communication" I mean two things. The first is being willing to talk about your feelings; to share your concerns, worries, and joys, and risk intimacy with your father. The second involves learning how to draw your father out.

Talking about your feelings requires that you put aside concerns about the social hierarchy and overcome your fear of being thought soft or effeminate. Take the chance of letting your father in on how you feel inside. It's especially important to be willing to reveal your tender feelings, since, as I pointed out earlier, it's easier for fathers and sons to be angry with one another than to be tender.

You cannot talk meaningfully about your feelings unless you're aware of them. This is often the most daunting barrier for men, who have choked back their feelings so habitually that they may have forgotten the knack of recognizing them. And, of course, you must first be able to recognize a feeling before you can possibly hope to express it to someone else. Form the habit of tuning in to your feelings and treating them with respect.

As a man, you must work especially hard to resist the cultural conditioning that invites you to invalidate or discount your feelings. Avoid saying things like, "I shouldn't feel this way!" or "It's silly to be upset over something so trivial!" or "It's wrong to feel like this!" Instead, accept your feelings as valid reflections of your inner state.

Only when you've come to accept the validity of your feelings does it become possible to talk about them with others.

When you do talk about them with other people, use "I-messages." For example, if a remark of your father's provokes annoyance, say, "I'm annoyed at what you said." Don't say, "You're annoying when you say things like that" or "Your comment annoyed me." This subtle difference may seem like mere word-play, but the psychological differences between "you-messages" and "I-messages" are far-reaching, as are the different effects each kind of message has on the relationship.

I-messages place responsibility for your feelings on you, which is where it belongs. By contrast, you-messages ("You never think of anybody but yourself!" or "You really make me sick!") place responsibility for how you feel outside yourself. They're judgmental, they sound harsh, and they're almost always counterproductive.

I-messages also reduce the likelihood of a defensive response. "You make me feel like I can never be good enough to please you" may be an accurate statement from your point of view. But it's unlikely to evoke an empathic response from your father, who is more likely to react by feeling helpless and annoyed. No one *makes* anyone else feel a particular way. On the other hand, "I feel like I can never be good enough to please you" is much more likely to provoke a helpful exchange. Your father is then free to say how *he* feels; and you have a much better chance of communicating something meaningful.

The point is to avoid you-messages. Avoid all labels and personal attacks. Use I-messages instead, placing the emphasis on your own reactions and feelings. The first column in the illustration below shows examples of statements that have been unproductively cast in the form of you-messages. In the second column, they have been recast in the form of I-messages.

*To a father who asks his son for advice then disregards it entirely:*

| You make me so angry—you're too stubborn to take my advice | I feel frustrated when you ask my advice then don't take it. |

*To a father who promises to make a cradle for his son's child, then fails to follow through:*

| | |
|---|---|
| Your promises are meaningless—Ben is going to be in high school before you finish that cradle. | I really feel hurt that you promised to make Ben a cradle but haven't followed through. |

*To a father who never took his son's concerns seriously:*

| | |
|---|---|
| You were always insensitive when it came to things I cared about. You made me so angry when you laughed at me. | I always felt so vulnerable with you when it came to things I really cared about. I used to feel so angry when you barely heard me out before telling me how I *should* be feeling. |

Notice that each I-message includes two components: a statement of how you feel, and an objective, judgment-free description of the other person's behavior that contains no labels or emotional language.

A third component, an explanation of your reaction, is optional. Suppose you harbor bad feelings because your father missed every school play you were ever in. Here are three ways you might let him know how you feel:

1. "You were wrong not to come to the plays I was in." This judgmental statement, a you-message, would most likely be experienced as a personal attack, and would almost certainly evoke a defensive response from your father.

2. "I was disappointed and angry when you didn't come to my plays." This is a perfectly acceptable I-message. Note that it does not include an explanation of why you reacted as you did. Such an explanation would shed even more light on what was going on inside you when he didn't attend.

3. "I was disappointed and angry when you didn't come to my plays, because I wanted you to acknowledge how hard I worked and to be proud of my accomplishments." (This is the most self-disclosing alternative, since it explicitly identifies the inner workings that accounted for your disappointment and anger.)

This last statement is an example of a full-blown I-message. It includes a statement of how you feel, an objective, judgment-free description of the other person's behavior, and an explanation of why you reacted the way you did.

### Draw Your Father Out

Intimacy requires that you talk about how you feel inside, and, clearly, I-messages help you do that. But initiating affective communication doesn't only mean sharing your own feelings. It also entails drawing your father out, encouraging him to talk about *his* feelings. Your goal here is to get to know as much as possible about your father's inner life. To succeed, you must help him feel safe opening up to you.

You can do this by questioning him—but not in a way that might cause him to feel uncomfortable. The tone in which you ask questions makes a big difference, as do the words you choose.

Few things are more unpleasant than a battery of personal questions asked without any real sensitivity, almost as a police interrogator might ask them. To set a more constructive tone, let your questions flow naturally from your conversation. Ask a thoughtful question and then really listen to your father's response. Ask your next question based on what he said, rather than simply waiting while he speaks until you can fire off another in a series of preplanned questions. One way to make this work is to preface all follow-up questions with comments that show your empathy for the emotions your father has conveyed.

For example, suppose your father recounts an experience that was obviously important and disappointing to him—say, the loss of a job. Perhaps his manner is halting and slightly embarrassed. Avoid simply barreling in with a host of questions: "Why'd you lose the job? How long had you been working there? What was Mom's reaction?" Instead, capture his emotional tone in the course of restating what you've understood; then ask your question. "You seemed to have a hard time just now talking about losing your job. Do you remember how you felt back then?" Even better, ask nothing and simply invite elaboration through your empathy and willingness to listen: "You seemed to have a hard time just now talking about losing your job. That must have been a difficult time for you." Then simply wait.

Not only your manner, but the words you choose can help draw your father out. Some questions can be too direct (for example, "Why did you hit me that time when I ran away from home?"). They can also invite intellectual rather than emotional discourse. It's better to facilitate a response with a question that specifically but sensitively targets your father's emotional reactions to a situation.

Suppose, for example, that as a high-schooler you were given an in-school suspension for some minor infraction. Your father overreacted, launching into an angry tirade and grounding you for a week. Rather than asking, "Why did you get so angry when I was suspended?" ask, "What was it about my getting suspended that upset you so much?" This form of the question discourages intellectualization and invites the kind of self-disclosing response that promotes dialogue.

Whatever the means by which you get your father to open up, make it a point to avoid judging or evaluating his feelings. Don't say, "You have no right to feel that way!" or "You shouldn't be angry!" Such remarks may be consistent with cultural conditioning; but they negate your father's feelings, and are a fail-proof way of bringing affective communication to a halt.

Even if you can't fathom why your father reacted as he did in a given situation, withhold your judgment. His feelings—no matter how illogical—are his own and need to be respected. The most you can do is to try as sensitively as possible to get to the bottom of his reactions. For example, if your father expresses what seems like inappropriate guilt about something, don't tell him not to feel guilty, but ask what it is about the situation he's described that evokes a guilty response. Your goal is not to dissuade him from feeling a particular way, but rather to understand the basis for his feeling.

## *Learn To Give and Receive Criticism Constructively*

More than once in this chapter, you've seen that fathers and sons have a hard time when either is critical of the other. Since any emotional encounter with your father may involve your critical feelings, I'll focus on these. The techniques presented here are equally applicable to fathers who find themselves in the position of needing to criticize their sons.

Giving and receiving criticism is tricky in any relationship. It's particularly difficult in the context of an emotion-charged, ongoing relationship. To criticize without doing harm, you need to have a clear idea of your purposes. And you need to follow specific guidelines.

What are the purposes of giving criticism in ongoing intimate relationships? There are three:

- To facilitate change in the person being criticized

- To communicate your reactions to his behavior

- To maintain his goodwill

Within a relationship between a father and son, any criticism that fails to meet all three goals must be considered unsuccessful.

### *Facilitate change*

Other people don't exist to satisfy your needs and wants. They have their own agenda; their needs may be entirely out of phase with yours. In every relationship, even the most satisfying ones, there are times when your wants and expectations are not fulfilled. When they aren't, you have the right, even the obligation, to convey your dissatisfaction and attempt to induce your partner in the relationship to change.

Here are three relevant examples:

- You object to the fact that your father doesn't show respect for your wife. You have the right, even the obligation, to tell him so. How can you hope that he'll change his behavior unless he knows that it's upsetting to you?

- Your father doesn't listen to your opinions or take them seriously. This bothers you. You have the right and obligation to convey your irritation. How can you expect him to begin responding as you'd like unless you let him know that you want him to change?

- Your father's past indifference to your academic accomplishments hurt you. He needs to know that. How else can he begin making up for it, perhaps by acknowledging your current achievements in ways that would be satisfying to you?

The question in all these cases, and a thousand more like them, is not whether to say anything. It's what to say and how. Suggestions about both follow.

### Convey your reactions

The second purpose of criticism is to let the object of your remarks know your inner responses to an objectionable behavior. It's not enough to convey your disapproval through silence or sulking, keeping your feelings bottled up. If you do, how can your father or anyone else know what's going on inside of you? Nor is it enough to simply react, hoping that the other person will correctly interpret the source of your actions. For example, if you are hurt by something your father says, it's not sufficiently communicative to blow up in a rage, curse him out, and bolt from the house, slamming the door behind you. He may easily misinterpret the source of your anger.

Both responses—sullen withdrawal and emotional acting-out—are typically male. Both can be very destructive. Neither lets the offender know precisely how to interpret or make sense of your behavior. In fact, what typically happens is that the original offense gets lost in the storm that surrounds your withdrawal or explosive outburst. The emotional emphasis is suddenly on what *you* have done rather than on what *he* has done. This scenario is all too familiar to many fathers and sons.

To improve matters, you must break the pattern that cultural conditioning has produced, substituting more effective communication strategies. This means conveying your reactions, identifying your feelings in response to your father's behavior, then putting those feelings into words—politely, forcefully, and unmistakably.

The guidelines offered in the discussion of I-messages are particularly useful here, since the same techniques should be applied in conveying your reactions to offensive behavior. Review those pages now if you have any questions about recognizing your feelings and learning how to talk about them.

### Maintain goodwill

In an ongoing relationship, it's particularly important to do more than simply "dump" your feelings on the other person. How many fathers and sons have become estranged for years because one or the other said deeply hurtful things and allowed the situation to end there?

Constructive criticism takes into account the feelings—especially the pride—of the recipient of the criticism. It enables him to save face—to change gracefully without having to concede that he has been wrong or foolish, or that his behavior has been reprehensible.

Well-cast criticism walks a narrow line between saying too little—thereby failing to get your feelings and needs across clearly—and inflicting psychological wounds. It may feel satisfying to inflict those wounds, particularly if you've been badly hurt yourself; however, the price paid for that vengeance far outweighs any temporary situation conferred.

The following guidelines will help you learn to criticize in a way that increases the likelihood that the recipient's goodwill will be maintained.

## Guidelines for Good Criticism

There are two guidelines you need to follow when offering criticism. The first is to focus on the behavior of the person being criticized, not his personality. The second is to convey understanding before criticizing.

### Address the behavior, not the person

Behavior can be changed; personality is a given. People can feel pretty devastated when criticized about something so closely identified with who they are, rather than what they've said or done.

By focusing on your father's behavior rather than his personality, you diminish his need to defend himself. Simultaneously, you increase the likelihood that he'll listen to your criticism.

Below are three situations that might occur between a father and son. In each one, the son is criticizing the father. After each situation, I provide an example of poorly worded criticism that is directed at the father's personality. Finally, I recast the message and give an example of criticism directed at his behavior.

As you read, you'll realize that the recast criticism is really a full-blown I-message—one that includes a description of the unwanted behavior, a statement of the son's feelings, and an explanation of why he reacted that way. Here again, the value of that tool shows itself.

*Situation 1:* A father promises to call his son, then fails to do so.

*Criticism Directed at the Person:* "You're undependable."

*Criticism Directed at the Behavior:* "When you promise to call and don't, I feel hurt. When you don't follow through on a promise, I feel like you just don't care."

*Situation 2:* During a talk with his adult son, a father displays a trait he's long had: he talks about himself at length but fails to pay any attention to his son's concerns.

*Criticism Directed at the Person:* "You've always been too wrapped up in yourself to pay any attention to what I have to say!"

*Criticism Directed at the Behavior:* "When you talk about yourself exclusively, I feel like I'm just your sounding board, not someone you care about. My concerns don't seem to matter to you at all."

*Situation 3:* A father has a long history of treating his son harshly, demanding a great deal of him and failing to acknowledge his son's efforts.

*Criticism Directed at the Person:* "You're a demanding, unappreciative man who doesn't know how to make people feel good about what they do."

*Criticism Directed at the Behavior:* "When you make demands and then fail to acknowledge my efforts, I get upset, because it feels like nothing I do is good enough."

### Convey understanding before criticizing

Even when they know they've made a mistake, people need to feel confident that their feelings are accepted and their intentions acknowledged before they'll accept criticism. No matter how upset or dissatisfied you are with your father, you have to acknowledge the validity of his feelings and intentions, even if what he did was horrible from your point of view.

Here are a few examples.

*Example 1.* A father sees that his married son is often tired. The father attributes his son's fatigue to the fact that he's working hard on the job while simultaneously trying to help his wife care for their newborn child. Out of concern, the father speaks to his daughter-in-law. She is hurt and tells her husband; in turn, he becomes upset. The son feels that he must convey the fact that he didn't appreciate Father's intrusiveness, and that he doesn't want him to intrude again. Rather than bawling out his father for trespassing on his personal life, the son needs to validate his father's intent and express understanding of his father's feelings (even gratitude for his concern). He must then make it clear that, despite everything, he would prefer that his father not behave that way in the future. His words might sound like this: "Dad, I appreciate your concern for me. I've been really tired lately, and it's nice to know you care enough to want to make things easier. But I have a real problem with your talking to Susan about it. Please trust me: I really can take care of myself. If I feel a need to say something to her, I will."

*Example 2.* A father and son begin speaking meaningfully about their shared past for the first time in a long while. In the course of one of their conversations, the father begins blaming himself, saying that he's caused the two of them to miss out on many years of a better relationship. The son feels that his father is being unfair to himself, but wisely avoids the tendency to invalidate his father's feelings by saying, "Don't feel guilty! It's not your fault." Instead, he acknowledges his father's feelings and intentions, then gently takes him off the hook by suggesting that they're equally to blame. His words might sound like this: "Dad, ever since we've begun talking today, I've noticed how quick you are to blame yourself for what went wrong between us. I know talking about all this is upsetting—it upsets me, too. And your wanting to take the blame is very generous. But the truth is, I think I'm as responsible as you are. After all, for a long time I sort of shut you out of my life."

*Example 3.* A father and son are talking about the past and father's extreme restrictiveness. The son has a long-standing resentment about his dad having imposed too many restrictions, and being entirely too rigid in enforcing them. As a father himself now, the son realizes that his dad's intentions were well-meaning; but he still needs to tell him how difficult it was to try to have a normal adolescence within the restrictive environment imposed by his father. Here's what the son might say: "You know, Dad, there were lots of times I really resented your rules. Now that I'm a father myself, I realize what a responsibility it is. I want you to know that I appreciate your intentions. But

I've got to tell you, it was rough! It's been hard to get over my anger about all those restrictions you imposed!"

## Reframing

One of the most effective techniques you can use to improve communication between you and your father is reframing. To understand how to use this tool, a little background is necessary.

I'm defining a frame in this context as a communication clue, usually nonverbal, that tells you how to interpret a verbal message. If someone says something that sounds serious but does so with a wink of his eye, you know it's a joke. He's framed the message as not what it seems by winking. Similarly, tone of voice, facial expression, posture, even the title used when addressing a person all frame a message. As the expression goes, "It's not what you say; it's how you say it!"

The choice of word is, of course, also important in terms of how a message is received. Many people can recall being addressed by their full name—"John Miller!" rather than the familiar "Johnny" or "Jack"—when being reprimanded by a parent.

When you hear a message, you react not only to the words but to the way in which they've been framed. Thus, if you were to turn to a person for help, you might feel that you had been either helped or patronized, depending on the helper's manner of responding.

Because of differences in the way people think, it's easy to misinterpret another person's intent in framing a message.

Here's a personal example. One day, I spoke to my wife about a problem I was having with a class I was teaching. My intent was to unburden myself a little and elicit her support and help in solving my problem. She responded sympathetically and completely spontaneously, "You poor thing!" But I bristled at her response, since it sounded to me as though she was being patronizing. For one thing, her sympathy seemed overdone; for another, she had reduced me to the status of a "thing." I frowned with annoyance and withdrew emotionally. (This was a response typical of a male, ever sensitive to a loss of status.) My reaction, in turn, hurt my wife, since she had meant to be genuinely supportive, and not patronizing, in her comment. It took some backtracking before we were able to get to the bottom of the misunderstanding and overcome the hard feelings that resulted.

What has all this to do with fathers and sons? Test your assumptions about your father's intent before you jump to any conclusions in your conversations with him. This may mean deferring your immediate emotional reactions to what he says— but that's okay. Your reaction may have been inappropriate to what was actually intended, just as my reaction to my wife's comment was inappropriate. Try also to be aware of the frames around what you say to your father. Are your words open to a negative interpretation that's unintended? Think about who's receiving the message, and the emotional baggage carried by your relationship. Then speak as clearly and with as much sensitivity and intention as you can. After all, if you're going to say something hurtful to someone, you want it to be intentional—not a horrible slip of the tongue.

You can also try talking about the *process* of communication between you: how is each of you talking to the other? What assumptions and feelings are being triggered by the conversation? For example, if you and your father are on a well-traveled road that has always led to misunderstanding, try talking about what's going on between you. Make the framing of your messages clear. If you feel as though the information you mean to convey in your message is being misunderstood, do not go on talking in the usual way. Instead, stop yourself and comment on the way your words are coming across. Say something along these lines: "Wait a minute!" Just now when I said, 'I wish things could've been different back then,' I wasn't attacking you or expressing disappointment in you. What I meant was that I'm sorry the two of us couldn't have enjoyed a better relationship a long time ago." This kind of reframing can break patterns of long standing and make new beginnings possible.

Alternatively, if you feel uncomfortable in the course of a conversation because of the way in which your father has framed his message, say so. For example, "Just now I began feeling like I was being lectured to. It felt like I was a kid again, and you were trying to 'set me straight.'" Talking about talk is a way of derailing automatic and often destructive ways of communicating.

## To Summarize

In this chapter you've learned how cultural conditioning contributes to the creation of barriers between fathers and sons. In the course of growing up, males are conditioned to see communication as a vehicle for maintaining their position in a hierarchy and imparting information—not as a way of establishing intimacy with their fellows. As a result, men are largely unable to express tender feelings directly or to give and receive nurturing.

You also learned how you can begin overcoming male communication barriers by initiating affective communication and giving and receiving criticism properly. You were introduced to "I-messages" as the most constructive way to share feelings and reactions. Finally, you learned to reframe messages to reduce the likelihood of misunderstanding and break long-standing destructive patterns of communication.

## Recommended Reading

Faber, A., and E. Mazlish (1980) *How To Talk So Kids Will Listen and Listen So Kids Will Talk.* New York: Avon.

Faber, A., and E. Mazlish (1987) *Siblings Without Rivalry.* New York: Avon.

Frank, J. (1973) *Persuasion and Healing* (rev. ed.). Baltimore: The Johns Hopkins University Press.

Gordon, T. (1977) *Leader Effectiveness Training.* New York: Bantam Books.

Gordon, T. (1970) *Parent Effectiveness Training.* New York: Wyden Books.

Hall, E. T. (1959) *The Silent Language.* Greenwich, CT: Fawcett Publications.

Keen, S. (1991) *Fire in the Belly.* New York: Bantam Books.

Miller, S. (1983) *Men and Friendship.* Los Angeles: Jeremey P. Tarcher, Inc.

Osherson, S. (1986) *Finding Our Fathers.* New York: Fawcett-Columbine.

Smith, M. (1973) *When I Say No I Feel Guilty.* New York: Bantam Books.

Tannen, D. (1990) *That's Not What I Meant.* New York: Ballantine Books.

Tannen, D. (1986) *You Just Don't Understand.* New York: Ballantine Books.

Torrey, E. F. (1973) *The Mind Game: Witchdoctors and Psychiatrists.* New York: Bantam Books.

# 9

# Overcoming the Consequences of Ineffective Fathering

In Chapters 5 and 6, you learned about the ways in which ineffective fathering affects a man's ability to work and love. If you are having difficulties in either area, the strategies presented in this chapter can help you. They are useful regardless of the type of ineffective fathering you received, and whatever the specific consequences have been on your work or intimate relationships.

Extremes of behavior—such as extreme neediness or extreme remoteness—can invariably be traced to what psychologists call your *inner monologue*. All too often, a person's inner monologue is peppered with negative and debilitating statements: you may incessantly think to yourself, "I'm worthless," or "My life has no meaning," or "I'm a lying, scheming bastard." Where do these statements come from, and why do they persist, even though they cast such a pall on people's lives and relationships? More to the point, how can you change them?

This chapter shows you how. First, you'll learn to monitor your inner monologue and uncover the self-statements that drive you. Second, you'll learn ways of scrutinizing and challenging your self-statements to expose the logical flaws and fallacies buried within them. Finally, you'll learn how to replace your negative self-statements with positive ones. Applied faithfully, this three-step strategy can help you overcome the programming that impedes your performance on the job and deprives you of satisfaction in intimate relationships.

## Monitor Your Inner Monologue

It's no accident that the children's book, *The Little Engine That Could* (Piper Watty New York: Platt and Murk, 1930) is a perennial favorite, for it captures a crucial truth: success often depends on what you tell yourself. Recall the story: a little engine must pull a heavy load up a steep hill. No one believes the engine can do it. But he is fiercely determined. He tells himself over and over, "I think I can! I think I can!" Huffing and puffing, he struggles up the steep hill. Eventually he succeeds.

Unfortunately, many men send themselves messages that work in precisely the opposite direction. Some tell themselves that they can't succeed. Others caution themselves against getting close to others. Still others send themselves fear-inspiring messages that discourage them from taking necessary risks.

Another group of men don't so much undermine their success as drive themselves beyond all reason toward extreme behavior. (They are like the Little Engine run amok, unable to stop straining even after pulling its load to the top of the hill.) They set impossible standards and tell themselves that they must meet them. Their manhood seems on the line every time they set out to achieve a goal. They counsel self-punishment in work situations, and emotional invulnerability in intimate relationships, since to them being tough is the only way to survive being close to another person.

The worst thing about destructive self-statements is that they are almost always completely unconscious and automatic. You are unaware of them because they pervade your thinking. They are not "called up," but rather assert themselves outside your conscious will.

Self-statements are learned habits of long standing, the products of conditioning. Although this means that they're deeply ingrained, it also means that there's reason to be hopeful: like any learned behavior, negative or destructive self-statements can be unlearned. You can almost literally reprogram yourself. Having changed your inner monologue, you can change the behavior that results from it.

The first step in changing your self-defeating inner monologue is to become aware of it. By making your self-statements conscious, you begin the process of changing them. It's not easy to tune in to your inner monologue, but it's possible with patience and determination.

How do you begin? There are two ways. By stepping back and observing yourself, you may be able to catch yourself in the act of making negative self-statements. Once you've succeeded in hearing your inner monologue, you will be ready to follow the recommendations that appear later in this chapter.

It's highly desirable to be able to catch yourself, but it's almost impossible to do so in the early stages of change. Because of this, you may have greater success exposing your self-statements retrospectively. That is, after you have behaved illogically, in an extreme or self-defeating way, ask yourself, "What was going through my mind? What thoughts were behind my feelings and behavior?" You then work to reconstruct the messages you were sending yourself at the time.

## Key Features of Self-Statements

Knowing some basic characteristics of self-statements can help you uncover your own. Here are the five most important characteristics to look for:

1. *Self-statements are invariably "must" statements in one form or another.* Some are obvious "musts." For example, "I must prove my worth!" "I must be treated with respect!" Others are less obvious: "I hate it when my superiors fail to acknowledge my contributions!" (This is a way of saying, "My contributions must be acknowledged!") Or again, "It would be disastrous if I failed!" (This is a way of saying, "I must succeed!")

As you learn to uncover your inner monologue, get into the habit of finding the "must"-statements buried in the messages you send yourself. Doing this will make it easier to challenge these statements later.

2. *All self-statements create urgency and anxiety.* Urgency typically results from the uncritically accepted belief that you'll be miserable unless you get what you want right away. It also results from believing that you can never be content if things remain as they are. For example, a man who believes that he must be treated respectfully will likely bristle at every imagined slight. His responses will be exaggerated, his anguish inappropriate to the situation. In his mind, it's urgent that everyone treat him respectfully all the time.

Self-statements create anxiety because they lead to the conviction that something awful will happen if the situation doesn't change. For example, a man might tell himself, "If I'm not respected by my boss [or perhaps "by my peers" or "by my subordinates"], I'll become the laughingstock of the office!" Anticipating such dire consequences feeds your feelings of unease.

3. *Self-statements appear to be logical.* In form and appearance even the most fallacious self-statements can seem logical. They often follow the cause-and-effect pattern of genuinely logical statements ("If I don't try, I can't succeed." "If the President's

budget passes, I'll pay more in taxes."). On the surface self-state-ments such as "If my boss speaks to me disrespectfully, I'll be the laughingstock of the office," seem to pass the test of logic. However, a logical format is not always a guarantee of ration-ality. Later you'll learn how to get beyond a false appearance of logic in critically evaluating and refuting your destructive self-statements.

4. *Self-statements are often truncated.* They take a complex idea or chain of associations and boil it down to a simple state-ment or prediction—for example, "I can't take it!" Such an inner remark probably has a complex history; it's a shorthand sum-mary of a person's past experience. Perhaps this man has had a bad time with a girlfriend who took advantage of his emo-tional vulnerability. As his current relationship progresses nor-mally and he begins to experience feelings of vulnerability, his past relationship flashes before his eyes. He summarizes all the hurt he experienced before and predicts (quite illogically) that he will be devastated again.

Because self-statements are truncated, they almost always gloss over important logical distinctions. This man's current part-ner is not the same person who hurt him in the past. There is absolutely no certainty or even likelihood that the outcome will be the same. Yet the statement "I can't take it!" uncritically im-plies that devastation will be the inevitable consequence of al-lowing himself to become emotionally vulnerable again.

By "fleshing out" your self-statements, you make them more accountable to the rules of reason and logic. Thus exposed, they are easier to test and challenge.

5. *Self-statements can be retrospective or predictive.* Retro-spective self-statements build illogical and unwanted bridges be-tween the past and the present. They turn back toward the past and suggest that it's being replayed in the present. The previous example is a perfect illustration of a retrospective self-statement. Here's another. A man criticized by a superior feels embarrassed and uncomfortable. He tells himself: "This feels just like my con-

versations with Dad. My boss is talking to me the way the old man used to. I can't let myself be treated like a child!" (The disguised "must" statement here is: "I must be treated with respect.")

Predictive self-statements foretell disaster. For instance, a man given a tough job assignment feels apprehensive and tells himself, "Oh God—I'm going to blow it again!" Another man starts a new job and notices that his boss has mannerisms similar to his father's. He tells himself, "I'll never be able to get along with this guy! He's too much like Dad!"

6. *Self-statements often combine thoughts and feelings.* For purposes of analysis, it's important to separate thoughts and feelings. Your job will be to concentrate on challenging the thought component of your negative self-statements.

Below are two examples of self-statements that combine thoughts and feelings. In both cases, the first part of the statement is the feeling; the second part is the thought. I've separated the two with a double slash ( / / ); the parentheses indicate which part is which. I've fleshed out the thought that appears in abbreviated form, followed by the "must" statement that's disguised in the thought.

"I'm too scared / / to manage this."

(Feeling)                    (Thought)
                             "I won't be able to
                             manage this."
                             (*I must succeed*)

"I hate / / being dumped on by authorities."

(Feeling)                    (Thought)
                             "I can't tolerate it when
                             people in authority treat
                             me badly."
                             (*I must be treated with
                             respect*)

## Your Self-Statements Are Unique to You

Self-statements differ from one person to the next as much as any other psychological characteristic. They are the product both of your past experience and your temperament. Often what your father has said to you can have a profound influence on your inner monologue.

As I mentioned in Chapter 5, the same sort of ineffective fathering can produce very different results. An indifferent and uncaring father can influence his son's self-statements in two directions, depending on the son's temperament. One son, sensitive and dependent, might respond by developing an urgent and undisguised need for recognition and acceptance. His self-statements might sound like this: "I must be recognized." "I must win the acceptance of superiors." "I must be treated with respect."

Another son, equally sensitive but less dependent, might conceal his need for recognition and acceptance. His self-statements might sound this way: "I mustn't show how much I need to be recognized." "I'll be damned if I'll beg for his acceptance!" "I don't need anybody's approval!"

Take a different situation. An overbearing father has two sons. One, adoring and eager to please, might expend tremendous energy trying to live up to the expectations that have been imposed. His self-statements might sound like this: "I must succeed!" "I must prove my worth by living up to the expectations of my superiors."

The other son, embittered by his inability to please his father, might develop a repertoire of self-statements that are rebellious in tone: "I can't stand it when superiors push me around!" "I'll be damned if I'll turn myself inside out to please my boss!"

## Record Your Self-Statements

Learn to identify your negative self-statements. This entails writing them down as soon as possible after thinking them.

Work to hone and revise these statements until they capture, as simply and directly as possible, the particular principle governing your behavior.

I recommend that you record your statements in a notebook. Initially, just date and record your thought, noting the underlying "must" statement. Briefly describe the circumstances. As your awareness increases, summarize the emotional situation or psychological context out of which the statement grew. Below are three sample notebook entries. The first two don't include reference to the psychological context; the third one does.

**Sample Entry 1**
**Date:** June 3
**Circumstances:** In the midst of preparing an important presentation for my boss

**Self-Statement:** "No way I'm going to be able to do this! (Underlying "must" statement: "I must succeed!")

**Sample Entry 2**
**Date:** June 4
**Circumstances:** After learning that one of my employees is planning to leave my company and take a job elsewhere

**Self-Statement:** "She can't do that! I need her here!" (Underlying "must" statement: "I must get all my needs met!")

**Sample Entry 3**
**Date:** August 12
**Circumstances:** After speaking with my teacher and feeling he'd dismissed my ideas

**Self-Statement:** "If I let him get away with this, it's all over!" (Underlying "must" statement: "I must be treated with respect!"

**Psychological Context:** "I've long felt that teachers don't take me seriously, and it's bothered me."

Record your statements for several weeks. During that time, make no attempt to analyze or change them. Just collect your data. You'll find that certain thoughts recur with remarkable regularity. These are the ones that constitute your repertoire of self-statements. Concentrate on these when following the steps detailed in the next sections of the chapter.

# Scrutinize Your Self-Statements

After you've collected a large sample of self-statements, begin examining the ones that occur most frequently. Your goal is to detect their logical flaws so that you can discredit and discard them. Accomplishing this objective requires two steps. First, ask yourself five general questions about the statement. These questions serve to challenge the general validity of your self-statements. Second, ferret out the specific logical fallacies that characterize each one.

## Step 1: Ask Five General Questions

1. *Am I looking at the whole picture?*   Often self-statements involve selective perceptions. You focus on only part of the picture, ignoring other parts that may be crucial in tempering your reaction to a situation.

For example, suppose a man with a troubled paternal relationship has a negative reaction to a superior. Some of his boss' mannerisms remind him of his father. He begins telling himself, "I'll never be able to get along with this guy! He's too much like the old man." This predictive self-statement is founded on fact: the boss does possess certain traits that are reminiscent of the man's father; but he fails to make certain crucial distinctions between them. It may be true that both his boss and his father are deliberate and precise in their speech. Both dress meticulously. They even sit and stand in a similar manner. However, his father rarely smiles, whereas his boss is characteristically pleasant and affable. Father rarely praises his son, while the boss makes it a point to compliment him on his work. And although the father uses his precise speech to embarrass others, the boss' precision is put to more constructive use. These crucial differences are glossed over in the subordinate's self-statement. Only by reminding himself to look at the whole picture can he detect the hidden fallacy in his thinking.

2. *What is the evidence for my belief?* Self-statements often involve the intellectual equivalent of "shooting from the hip." They often go far beyond the data you've actually observed, and extend your thinking in ways that are irrational.

One client told me that he prided himself on his ability to size up co-workers. In a new position, he'd carefully observe others, then come to a judgment about whether or not they could be trusted. Although he knew that the amount of time he spent on his observations was short, he invariably clung to his initial impression, allowing it to determine his behavior toward each individual. "We'll work well together," he'd remark of one man. Of another he might say, "I'm bound to be burnt by him!" This inordinate trust in first impressions became a kind of fortune-telling that blinded him to other possibilities.

Another client told me that each time he met an appealing woman, he told himself, "I won't be able to sustain this relationship. She'll lose interest in me very quickly." Although these predictions had no basis in reality, they often became self-fulfilling prophecies.

In both cases, the self-statements were based on inadequate evidence. But both men believed their thoughts with such conviction that they served to create the very scenarios the men feared, rather than reflecting reality. Changing their thinking required scrutinizing the statements and exposing the paucity of evidence on which they were based. Only then was it possible for these men to suspend their preconceptions and let facts rather than prejudice determine their attitudes. I encouraged them to revise their self-statements on the basis of additional data. When this was done, they were decidedly more capable of responding to the actual situations and the real people they confronted.

*3. Is this always true?*  Self-statements typically have a definitive, unequivocal quality to them. They sound as though they articulate a profound and inviolable truth.

One man carried around the belief that authorities can't be relied on. "In the end," he reasoned, "they'll serve their own interests at my expense." Another client explained why he preferred to work for female bosses by saying, "I don't get along well with male bosses." A third had difficulty with certain male superiors who were brighter than he and more focused in their work: "Men like him always wind up losing respect for me."

All three statements seem unassailable. "This is simply the way things are," they seem to say. By asking the question, "Is this always true?" I encouraged the men to sift through their past experiences and look for evidence that ran counter to their beliefs. All three were able to recall at least one instance that disproved the self-statement in question. It then became possible for them to see their thinking in a new light. If they did not toss the statements out entirely, at least they called them into question.

*4. Must things turn out as I expect?*  Predictive self-statements very rarely admit more than one outcome. "She'll never forgive me now!" thought one man after he'd said deeply hurtful things during an argument with his girlfriend. "I'll fail for sure!" said another who'd been given a particularly challenging assignment by his boss.

In both cases, a quality of inevitability characterized their statements. Desirable or even acceptable outcomes were completely excluded from their thoughts. They failed to consider possibilities that, speaking logically, were at least as probable as the dire consequences they foresaw.

The man who said, "She'll never forgive me now!" failed to consider the possibility that the woman might well understand his behavior if he offered a sincere apology and explained why he had reacted so strongly.

Similarly, the man who was convinced he'd fail did not take these facts into account. His prediction was based on experiences that occurred in the distant past: as an adolescent and young adult, he'd been given tasks he was not equipped to handle and was unable to complete successfully. Since then, he had acquired experience, skill, and insight that made the task he'd been given by his boss well within his range of competency. It was not only possible but extremely likely that he would succeed.

In both cases, by asking themselves, "Must things turn out as I expect?" the men were able to revise their thinking and defeat their negative self-statements.

5. *Why am I reacting in this illogical way?* Or again, *Where is this reaction coming from?* These questions are particularly useful when you've caught yourself in the act of behaving irrationally. If time has passed, the questions need to be recast as follows: "Why did I react in that illogical way? Where did my reaction come from?" Both versions invite you to search for the psychological underpinnings of your self-statements.

One man I met entered therapy not at all certain that he wanted to continue working in the corporate world. He felt confined and out of place, he said, and really would prefer to work for himself. I suggested that he begin exploring options, and mentioned specific books and other resources that might help him in his task. When we next meet, he reported that he'd done none of the reading and didn't follow through on any of the suggestions I'd made. He was unable to say why—just that he'd been unable to do even part of the assignment.

Exploration revealed that his unwillingness was based on his need to resist all directives given him by male authorities. "If I comply, I'll lose my self-respect" was the self-statement that lay beneath his opposition. His resistance could be traced back to a troubled relationship with a domineering father. He had been so enraged by his father's behavior that he irrationally saw any directives given him by any authority as demeaning: he was bound to resist. The recognition made it possible for him to complete the homework assignment over the next several weeks.

## Step 2: Identify the Specific Logical Fallacies in Your Self-Statements

Cognitive therapists have identified 14 common distortions in thinking that frequently make their way into self-statements. By uncovering these logical distortions, you can challenge your thinking and revise it.

*All-or-Nothing Thinking* (also known as *Polarized Thinking*). When you fall victim to this distortion, you eliminate all shades of gray and see complex realities in simple black-and-white terms. For example, "I'm so stupid! I bungle everything I every try."

*Blaming.* When your self-statements involve blaming yourself or others, they make it virtually impossible to learn from your experience. After a battle with his fiancée, one man told himself, "This entire argument is my fault. Sheryl tried to tell me what she wanted, but I just didn't listen!"

*Catastrophizing* (also known as *Awfulizing*). This fallacy is characteristic of predictive self-statements. You predict that your behavior will cause the most horrible consequences. At the same time, you inflate the importance or severity of an event or its outcomes. For example, "If I don't get promoted, I'll be so embarrassed I'll have to leave the company."

*Minimizing.* When your self-statements are distorted by this fallacy, you downplay your past successes and accomplishments, thereby ensuring a lack of confidence in the present. For example, you may tell yourself, "I may have been able to convince Jim, but he's a soft touch! I'll never be able to convince Adrian!"

*Fortune-Telling.* This fallacy is at the heart of predictive self-statements. It involves foretelling the future without having any logical basis for your prediction. For example, "I'm going to fall on my face if I try to sell this idea to my boss."

*Labeling.* This is just what it sounds like. Instead of looking at past failures as opportunities to learn or grow, you use them as excuses to pin labels on yourself. For example, "I've always been a jerk and I'm still a jerk!"

*Mental Filtering* (also known as *Tunnel Vision*). When your self-statements include this distortion, you overlook positive aspects of your personality or past experience and focus instead on the negative. Mental filtering is particularly common in retrospective self-statements. For example, you may have had several satisfying love relationships, but the one that was disastrous is the only one you recall.

*Mind-Reading.* This distortion is characteristic of self-statements that purport to capture how others are thinking or feeling. "He's probably wondering why he ever hired me." Or again, "She's completely bored by what I'm saying."

*Overgeneralization.* When you take a particular experience and see it as having implications far beyond the dictates of reason, you've overgeneralized. This distortion is quite common in retrospective self-statements. For example, "I was such a drip as a teenager!"

*"Should" Statements.* You're victimized by this distortion when you either second-guess your behavior or impose unrealistic expectations on yourself. For example, "I shouldn't even be in this job! I just can't handle it." Or again, "I should be able to do this much more quickly."

*Selective Interpretation.* This distortion is a bit like quoting someone out of context. You select a particular response or comment and fixate on it, ignoring the larger context within which it occurred. For example, if your boss is momentarily displeased with you and glances harshly at you or speaks angrily, you conclude that he altogether dislikes you.

*Personalization.* You know you're the victim of this distortion if, in your self-statements, you take things entirely too personally. For example, if someone fails to return your call, you assume it means that you're of no importance to him or her. (In fact, a host of other explanations are possible: the person may be tied up, the message may have been lost, he or she may be preparing information for you, and so on.)

*Emotional Reasoning* (also known as *Subjective Reasoning and Reasoning With Your Heart*). When your self-statements include this fallacy, you allow your subjective reactions to shape your perceptions of reality. For example, "When I talk to this guy, I feel like I did when I used to try to talk with Dad; he's just like my father!"

*Over-Responsibility.* This distortion frequently occurs in self-statements by which you impose responsibility on yourself for things you can't cause or haven't done. For example, "It's my fault that her article wasn't accepted for publication. If I'd been more thorough in my criticism, it would have been accepted." Or, "If I don't do this job just right, the entire department will look bad."

To apply what you've just learned, here's what I recommend you do. Begin by writing down the self-statement you found yourself making most frequently. Beneath it, write the five general questions described in Step 1. Recall that these questions are designed to help you challenge the general validity of your self-statement. Here are the questions again:

1. Am I looking at the whole picture?

2. What is the evidence for my belief?

3. Is this always true?

4. Must things turn out as I expect?

5. Why am I reacting in this illogical way? Where is this reaction coming from?

Answer all that are pertinent.

Next use the 14 questions below as a guideline to help you determine which of the logical distortions are operative in your self-statement.

1. Does this statement reduce a complex reality to black-and-white or all-or-nothing alternatives?

2. In my self-statement, do I react to a setback or disappointment by allocating blame rather than seeing it as an opportunity to learn?

3. Does my statement forecast some negative outcome I fear, and couch it as a catastrophe I couldn't survive?

4. Does the statement downplay or trivialize my accomplishments?

5. Does the statement predict some unwanted outcome without relying on any solid evidence for the prediction?

6. In my self-statement, do I call myself or others names or describe myself or others in unflattering terms?

7. In my statement, are my past successes and accomplishments ignored, and does it focus instead on past failures?

8. Does the statement include logical-sounding conclusions about how others might be thinking or feeling, but lack any solid evidence?

9. Does the statement generalize from a specific example to a conclusion that is not supported by the facts?

10. Does my self-statement impose unrealistic expectations on me, or involve second-guessing my behavior?

11. In my statement, is some event or experience taken out of context and used as a basis for a conclusion that isn't supported by the larger body of facts?

12. Does the statement explain events by reference to others' personal reactions to me, without considering other reasonable explanations?

13. Does my self-statement arrive at conclusions about reality based solely on how I feel?

14. In my self-statement, do I take responsibility for something I haven't done or could not have caused?

Look at the example below. It illustrates the format for this activity. Not every logical fallacy is pertinent for every self-statement.

## Sample Worksheet
### *Analyzing Your Self-Statements*

**Self-statement:** *When I talk to this guy, I feel like I did when I used to talk with Dad! He's just like the old man.*

**Questions to challenge the general validity of my self-statement:**

1. Am I looking at the whole picture?

   *This statement asserts that the person I'm talking to is just like Dad. I'm basing that conclusion on how I feel. But I haven't looked at the man's entire range of behavior. He's more friendly overall, and he's different from Dad in that he doesn't need to put others down. I may feel differently talking to him at other times and under different circumstances.*

2. What is the evidence for my belief?

   *I have no real evidence other than the fact that when I talk with him, I feel the way I did when I used to talk with Dad.*

3. Is this always true?

> *First of all, it may happen that I don't always feel that way when we talk. Maybe the feelings only happen in some contexts (for example, when I'm defending myself or making a request) and not others. Second, even if I do always feel the same way, that doesn't necessarily mean that the man is just like Dad.*

4. Must things turn out as I expect?

   *Not applicable.*

5. Why am I reacting in this illogical way? Where is this reaction coming from?

   > *When I was a kid, Dad could never give me a task to do without sarcastically implying that I didn't carry my load around the house. I used to feel resentful and angry because I knew he was wrong: I did do my share! Now I'm feeling the same way when my boss gives me work to do. And I'm saying that because I feel the way I did when I used to talk with Dad, my boss must be just like him. That's just not so! I'm the one who has the problem here!*

### Specific Logical Distortions

1. Does this statement reduce a complex reality to black-and-white or all-or nothing alternatives?

   *No*

2. In my self-statement, do I react to a setback or disappointment by allocating blame rather than seeing it as an opportunity to learn?

   *No*

3. Does my statement forecast some negative outcome I fear, and couch it as a catastrophe I couldn't survive?

*No*

4. Does the statement downplay or trivialize my accomplishments?

    *No*

5. Does the statement predict some unwanted outcome without relying on any solid evidence for the prediction?

    *No*

6. In my self-statement, do I call myself or others names or describe myself or others in unflattering terms?

    *No*

7. In my statement, are my past successes and accomplishments ignored, and does it focus instead on past failures?

    *No*

8. Does the statement include logical-sounding conclusions about how others might be thinking or feeling, but lack any solid evidence?

    *No*

9. Does the statement generalize from a specific example to a conclusion that is not supported by the facts?

    *No*

10. Does my self-statement impose unrealistic expectations on me, or involve second-guessing my behavior?

    *No*

11. In my statement, is some event or experience taken out of context and used as a basis for a conclusion that isn't supported by the larger body of facts?

    *No*

12. Does the statement explain events by reference to others' personal reactions to me, without considering other reasonable explanations?

    *No*

13. Does my self-statement arrive at conclusions about reality based solely on how I feel?

    *Yes! I'm saying that, because I feel a certain way (the way I used to when I talked with Dad), then this man must be just like my father. This is a clear example of forming conclusions about others based on how I feel.*

14. In my self-statement, do I take responsibility for something I haven't done or could not have caused?

    *No*

Finally, for each flaw you've discovered in your self-statement, formulate a logical comeback. Your response must be a compelling refutation of the fallacy involved.

Using the example above, the refutation would read as follows:

**Questions and refutations to challenge the general validity of my self-statement:**

1. Am I looking at the whole picture?

    **Fallacy:** *This statement asserts that the person I'm talking to is just like Dad. I'm basing this conclusion on how I feel. But I haven't looked at the man's entire range of behavior. He's more friendly overall, and he's different from Dad in that he doesn't need to put others down. I may feel differently talking to him at other times and under different circumstances.*

    **Logical comeback:** *The fact that I feel this way doesn't prove that the man is just like Dad. He may be very different. My feelings are not a reliable indicator of* *what he's really like. Something about the situation we both find ourselves in may be bringing out those feelings in me. The entire problem may be mine and not his! It is grossly unfair (to him and to me) to judge him on the basis of something as subjective as my feelings.*

2. What is the evidence for my belief?

   **Fallacy:** *I have no real evidence other than, when I talk with him, I feel the way I did when I used to talk with Dad.*

   **Logical comeback:** *The total lack of evidence is sufficient reason to ignore what I'm telling myself.*

3. Is this always true?

   **Fallacy:** *Sometimes our exchanges are completely benign. I just tend to remember our unpleasant exchanges more.*

   **Logical comeback:** *It's absurd to conclude that he's just like my father. I have no objective evidence whatsoever. It would be even more absurd to conclude that he will always behave like my father, or that in every interaction I have with him I'm destined to feel the way I did when I used to talk with Dad.*

4. Must things turn out as I expect?

   *Not applicable.*

5. Why am I reacting in this illogical way? Where is this reaction coming from?

   **Fallacy:** *When I was a kid, Dad could never give me a task to do without implying that I didn't carry my load in the household. I used to feel resentful and angry because I knew he was wrong: I did do my share! Now I'm feeling the same way when my boss* *gives me work to do. And I'm saying that because I feel the way I did when I used to talk with Dad, my boss must be just like him. That's just not so! I'm the one who has the problem!*

**Logical comeback:** *The only rational thing I can do in this situation is realize that my emotional reactions are way off the mark. They are the product of my past and have no place in the present situation, which is unique. I have to deal with it on this level.*

### Specific Logical Distortions
1-12. *Not applicable.*

13. Does my self-statement arrive at conclusions about reality based solely on how I feel?

**Fallacy:** *Yes. I'm saying that, because I feel a certain way (the way I used to when I talked with Dad), then this man must be just like my father. This is a clear example of forming conclusions about others based on how I feel.*

**Logical comeback:** *The man may be very different from my father. I need to suspend my judgment and not allow my feelings to dictate how I respond to him. In reality, the likelihood of any two men being exactly alike is virtually nil. It's my own feelings that need attending to here! If I'm going to behave rationally in this relationship, I have to examine why I'm reacting this way.*

Photocopy the blank worksheet that follows (I suggest that you make several copies). Fill out one worksheet for each self-statement you've identified.

# Worksheet
## *Analyzing Your Self-Statements*

**Self-statement:** _____

_____

**Questions and refutations to challenge the general validity of my self-statement:**

1. *Am I looking at the whole picture?*
   Have I taken all relevant information into account in coming to my conclusion? If not, what information have I failed to take into account? _____

   _____

   _____

   _____

   If I step back and consider all pertinent information, might I come to a different conclusion? What might it be?_

   _____

   _____

   _____

2. *What is the evidence for my belief?*
   Upon what evidence is my belief based? _____

   _____

   _____

   How much of my evidence is objectively verifiable? _____

   _____

   _____

   Which pieces of evidence are based on objectively verifiable facts? _____

   _____

   _____

   _____

How much of my evidence is based on my fears or suspicions? _____

_____

_____

_____

Which pieces of evidence are based on my fears or suspicions? _____

If I applied strict tests of objectivity in judging my evidence, would I arrive at a different belief? What might it be? _____

_____

_____

_____

3. *Is this always true?*
Have I invested my belief with a sort of inviolability, as though it captured an eternal, unvarying truth? If so, is that a reasonable thing for me to have done?_____

_____

_____

_____

Under what circumstances might my belief be untrue or only partially true?_____

_____

_____

_____

4. *Must things turn out as I expect?*
Objectively speaking, what is the probability that the prediction embodied in my self-statement will come to pass? _____

_____

_____

_____

What factors could contribute to a different outcome, and what influence might those factors exert? _____

_____

_____

_____

5. *Why am I reacting in this illogical way? Where is the reaction coming from?*
   Why might I have come to this conclusion? _____

   _____

   _____

   _____

   What experiences of mine might have led me to this belief? _____

   _____

   _____

   _____

   Why does this point of view seem so compelling to me?

   _____

   _____

   _____

   **Specific logical distortions.** (Check "yes" or "no." If your answer is yes, use the space below the question to show how the statement is fallacious.)

1. Does this statement reduce a complex reality to black-and-white or all-or-nothing alternatives?
   ☐ Yes  ☐ No
   **Fallacy:**_____

   _____

   _____

   _____

   **Logical comeback:** _____

   _____

   _____

   _____

2. In my self-statement, do I react to a setback or disappointment by allocating blame rather than seeing it as an opportunity to learn?

☐ Yes   ☐ No

**Fallacy:**_____

_____

_____

_____

**Logical comeback:** _____

_____

_____

_____

3. Does my statement forecast some negative outcome I fear and couch it as a catastrophe I could not survive?

☐ Yes   ☐ No

**Fallacy:**_____

_____

_____

_____

**Logical comeback:** _____

_____

_____

_____

4. Does the statement downplay or trivialize my accomplishments?

☐ Yes   ☐ No

**Fallacy:**_____

_____

_____

_____

**Logical comeback:** _____

_____

_____

_____

5. Does the statement predict some unwanted outcome without relying on any solid evidence for the prediction?

☐  Yes   ☐  No

**Fallacy:**_____

_____

_____

**Logical comeback:** _____

_____

_____

_____

6. In my self-statement, do I call myself or others names or describe myself or others in unflattering terms?

☐  Yes   ☐  No

**Fallacy:**_____

_____

_____

**Logical comeback:** _____

_____

_____

_____

7. In my statement, are my past successes and accomplishments ignored, and does it focus instead on past negatives?

☐  Yes   ☐  No

**Fallacy:**_____

_____

_____

**Logical comeback:** _____

_____

_____

_____

8. Does the statement include logical-sounding conclusions about how others might be thinking or feeling, but lack any solid evidence?

☐ Yes   ☐ No

**Fallacy:**_____

_____

_____

_____

**Logical comeback:** _____

_____

_____

_____

9. Does the statement generalize from a specific example to a conclusion that is not supported by the facts?

☐ Yes   ☐ No

**Fallacy:**_____

_____

_____

_____

**Logical comeback:** _____

_____

_____

_____

10. Does my self-statement impose unrealistic expectations on me, or does it involve second-guessing my behavior?

☐ Yes   ☐ No

**Fallacy:**_____

_____

_____

_____

**Logical comeback:** _____

_____

_____

_____

11. In my statement, is some event or experience taken out of context and used as the basis for a conclusion that isn't supported by the larger body of facts?

☐ Yes  ☐ No

**Fallacy:**_____

_____

_____

_____

**Logical comeback:** _____

_____

_____

_____

12. Does the statement explain events by reference to others' personal reactions to me, without considering other reasonable explanations?

☐ Yes  ☐ No

**Fallacy:**_____

_____

_____

_____

**Logical comeback:** _____

_____

_____

_____

13. Does my self-statement arrive at conclusions about reality based solely on how I feel?

☐ Yes  ☐ No

**Fallacy:**_____

_____

_____

_____

**Logical comeback:** _____

_____

_____

_____

14. In my self-statement, do I take responsibility for something I haven't done or could not have caused?

    ☐ Yes  ☐ No

    **Fallacy:**_____

    _____

    _____

    _____

    **Logical comeback:** _____

    _____

    _____

    _____

# Replace Your Negative Self-Statements With Positive Counterstatements

Once you've identified your self-statements and uncovered their logical flaws, you've weakened their power over you. There remains only one step: to begin replacing these thoughts with more constructive and positive ones.

Your counterstatements will be unique to you, since they must respond to your own particular self-statements. Therefore it's impossible to tell you exactly how to phrase them. However, there *are* seven criteria for well-fashioned counterstatements, regardless of their content:

- Each counterstatement should be stated in positive terms. Rather than saying, "I don't have to prove my worth as a person by being financially successful," say, "I have worth as a person regardless of whether I'm a financial success."

- Your counterstatement should include the first-person pronoun ("I"). There are two reasons for this. First, "I" statements place responsibility for outcomes and feelings on you. Second, they create a sense of immediacy. Instead of saying, "He's got to acknowledge my hard work and successes," say, "I can feel good about my hard work and success, whether or not he acknowledges them."

- Your comeback should be directly responsive to the underlying meaning of your original self-statement. For instance, take the thought, "She'll probably be uninterested in me!" The underlying fear in the statement is that she'll find you undesirable and unattractive, and that you'll feel humiliated and awful when she shows no interest in you. Your positive counterstatement might sound like this: "I'm a reasonably attractive guy with some desirable qualities. That won't change even if she isn't interested in me. I'd like it if she were, but I'll still be attractive and desirable, regardless of how she reacts."

- Your statement should be as simple and straightforward as possible. Avoid constructing counterstatements that are overly complex or burdened with too many qualifiers. "I'd like it if I always got my way, but it isn't essential to my happiness," is preferable to, "I know it's not realistic to expect to get my way all the time (and especially when the person whose cooperation I must get is a difficult individual overall), but I can certainly be happy on those occasions when I don't."

- Sometimes including the background of your counterstatement makes it more believable and compelling. When this is the case, a succinct summary should be included. For example, suppose you habitually freeze when you face a challenge. As a youngster, your father used to give you tasks that were too difficult for you. You failed so many times that even now, as an adult, each time you face a challenge you tell yourself, "I'll never be able to complete this assignment!" Your counterstatement might read like this: "As a child I was often unsuccessful at tasks I was given because I lacked the experience, skill, and insight to complete them. But I'm not a child any more. I have all the resources I need to complete this task, and I'll do it successfully."

- The wording of your statement should allay feelings of urgency and anxiety. Formulate it so that it takes the pressure off you. For example, when a predictive self-statement foretells disaster ("I'm going to give a lousy presentation, make a fool of myself, and wind up losing my job!"), your counterstatement should establish that the dire consequences foreseen are unlikely to come about. Here's a well-formulated counterstatement along these lines: "I've been asked to make this presentation because I'm more familiar with the subject matter than anyone else in the company. If I prepare thoroughly, I have every reason to expect I'll succeed. The likelihood of my making a fool of myself is virtually nil. Even if things do go poorly, I'm certainly not going to lose my job over it! My overall job performance, which is excellent, is much more important than how I do on a single presentation."

- Compose a statement you can really believe in. Suppose you're given a difficult task by your boss and you're genuinely unsure about your ability to complete it successfully. Your original self-statement might be, "I'm going to fail." Hollow reassurance ("I'm going to succeed") won't have much of a beneficial effect. Better to formulate a realistic counterstatement you can believe: "I'm going to take my time, learn what I must do to complete this task successfully, formulate a plan, and implement it carefully."

## Write Down Your Counterstatements

Once you've formulated your positive counterstatements, write them down and compile them neatly. One way to do this is by using index cards. On one side of each card, write your original self-statement; on the other side, write your counterstatement. Get into the habit of reading your counterstatements at least once daily. Review them as often as necessary whenever you're in a situation that would ordinarily evoke one or more of your undesirable self-statements.

Another strategy is to record your positive counterstatements on audio-tape, leaving several seconds between each one. Once or twice a day, when you're relaxed and can be assured of no interruptions, play the tape, allowing the new messages to penetrate deeply into your mind.

Remember—your self-statements are mental habits, the product of many years of conditioning. Don't expect them to disappear quickly. It will require discipline and practice to change your inner tune. Invariably, however, your hard work will be rewarded. Don't quit and revert to your old, self-defeating ways of thinking.

## To Summarize

Ineffective fathering leaves a legacy of negative self-statements that can adversely affect your behavior in work situations and intimate relationships. These statements, which are automatic and unconscious, constitute an inner monologue that can undermine your belief in yourself or drive you to extremes of behavior. In this chapter, you've learned ways of making your inner monologue fully conscious, challenging your self-statements, and replacing them with positive counterstatements.

## Recommended Reading

Block, D. (1990) *Words That Heal: Affirmations and Meditations for Daily Living.* New York: Bantam Books.

Bourne, E. J. (1990) *The Anxiety and Phobia Workbook.* Oakland, California: New Harbinger Publications, Inc.

Burns, D. (1981) *Feeling Good.* New York: Signet.

Cox, L. N., ed. (1987) *Dear Dad.* San Francisco: Saybrook Publishing Co.

Ellis, A., and R. W. Harper. (1975) *A New Guide to Rational Living.* North Hollywood, California: Wilshire Book Co.

Helmstetter, S. (1982) *The Self-Talk Solution.* New York: Pocket Books.

Woolfalk, R. L. and F. C. Richardson. (1978) *Stress, Sanity, and Survival.* New York: Signet.

# 10

# Looking Toward the Future

Over the past few decades, a number of changes have begun to have a positive impact on the father-son relationship. While certain immutable realities will continue to impose their limits, a gradual improvement in the conditions and circumstances surrounding fatherhood is underway.

## Constants in the Father-Son Tie

Although there are many opportunities for change and improvement in what happens between fathers and sons, there are four characteristics of their relationship that will never change. These should be kept firmly in mind while you read about the positive changes that are in the works.

- For biological reasons, sons will never be as close to their father as they are to their mother. The physical connection between mother and son is unique. Although much can be done to enable fathers and sons to approximate the psychological bond between mothers and sons, the biological connection can never be simulated.

- Fathers will always vary temperamentally and as a result of their life experience. This is bound to affect the way they behave as fathers. (Of course, the same is true of mothers). Three key variables will continue to exert influence.

  First, there will always be temperamental differences among men. Some are going to be temperamentally better suited than others to the role of father.

  Second, some men will feel more keenly than others the financial burdens associated with their role as father. Few fathers are the only source of family income nowadays; nevertheless, for some men the economic responsibility will have the effect of curbing their involvement with their children.

  Third, a man's experience with children before becoming a father will have an effect on how comfortable he feels in his role as caretaker. A man who is an older sibling and who cared for younger children will be more familiar with the responsibilities and skills associated with his role. There is a strong likelihood that as a result he will feel—and be—closer to his son.

- Time will always have a major impact on the relationship between fathers and sons, ensuring that the two are forever out of synch.

  Because of the differences in age, the needs, concerns, and interests of fathers and sons will rarely coincide. The best they can hope for is that their needs may complement each other's some of the time. Similarly, a father's age at the time of his son's birth will affect the relationship they have.

- Psychological influences will continue to affect fathers and sons, no matter how enlightened fathers may be. A son will always spark ambivalence, since he represents the father's mortality, and there is an extremely strong likelihood that the son will outdo his father in significant ways.

These four constants will always impose limits on the closeness that fathers and sons can enjoy. Nevertheless, important changes in the cultural and societal context of their relationship have already begun to have a positive impact and will probably continue to do so.

# Changes in the Context of the Father-Son Relationship

Two major changes have begun to have an effect on what happens between fathers and sons. One is cultural, the other demographic.

## Cultural Change: The New Vision of Masculinity

Cultures are living things. Like all life, they evolve; so do their basic components. The roles men and women play, and the expectations they must meet in order to be identified as male or female, constitute one such component of culture.

Over the past few decades, the concept of masculinity has been undergoing revision. This shows itself in popular views of the male hero, and in changing attitudes toward male livelihood. The effects of these changes on a man's fathering behavior are many and far-reaching.

## Heroes

The popular stereotype of the male hero has always been an individual alone and apart, strong, silent, and emotionally invulnerable. From the Knights of the Round Table to John Wayne, these heroes all were noted for their strength, physical prowess, and emotional detachment. Unfortunately, in the course of demonstrating their masculinity, such men often sacrificed gentleness, expressiveness, and responsiveness, which have traditionally been considered to be female characteristics. Many of the rest of us followed in their footsteps—or at least aspired to.

Only lately, this view of the male hero has begun to change. Increasingly, a man can reveal his feminine side without in any way putting his masculinity at risk. Many contemporary male heroes are much less emotionally isolated than their counterparts from the past. Heroes no longer need to be physically overpowering or emotionally untouchable. They can be soft, expressive, vulnerable, and tender. Such heroes are embodied by the character Hawkeye in the television version of "M-A-S-H," by Bill Cosby's Dr. Huxtable, and Dustin Hoffman's character in "Kramer vs Kramer," to name just a few (one also thinks of Kevin Costner in "Dances With Wolves").

This broadening of the range of behaviors available to heroic men has far-reaching implications. It affords ordinary men an opportunity to behave in ways that were not possible before. If a hero can display such traits as vulnerability and tenderness, then so can average men. So can fathers.

## Livelihood

A major shift has occurred in society's views of a man's role and responsibility as a provider. Traditionally, men were expected to pledge primary allegiance to the company or corporation for which they worked, often at the expense of involvement in their family. Those who did were generously rewarded for their loyalty. By contrast, men whose primary allegiance was to their families were considered odd.

While this way of thinking hasn't disappeared entirely, it has changed dramatically. An ever larger number of employers are offering paternity leave to new fathers. Many companies have policies that permit an employee who doesn't want to disrupt his family life to turn down a promotion requiring relocation.

Still another major attitudinal shift has occurred. Once emphasis was almost exclusively placed on the economic good generated by a man's livelihood. Little, if any, attention was paid to the impact of his work on the physical or social environment. For example, manufacturing was considered good regardless of its adverse effects on the environment. Similarly, people were viewed as objects (the term "human resources" is a legacy of that view) to be exploited and discarded when no longer useful.

Lately, there's been an important change in the perspective from which a man's manner of earning a living is viewed. Economic and financial success are no longer the only criteria by which a man's work life is judged. More and more people consider it backward and unacceptable to devote one's life to exploiting the environment and other people for personal gain, just as the acquisition of wealth for its own sake is no longer considered chic. It's now widely accepted that a person's work should have a socially positive value.

This change in values has not taken place in a vacuum. It is part of a broader evolutionary trend that has had the effect of humanizing the concept of masculinity. If a man can't use his environment for his personal gain, neither can he "use" his wife as a baby machine. He is an equal partner not only in the creation of life, but in the responsibility for the care of children his sperm engender.

### Consequences

As a direct result of these and other changes in the concept of masculinity, men are being given much more latitude in their relationship with their sons.

*The ethics of independence, self-sufficiency, and isolation are be-
ing replaced by the ethics of family and community.* More and more,
the importance of connectedness and interdependence is being
widely recognized. Intimacy, cooperation, and emotional bond-
ing hold more sway among many men than toughness, distance,
and emotional invulnerability.

As a result, many of today's young fathers are better able
than their own fathers to respond emotionally to their sons.
Fewer fathers than ever are choosing to relinquish the role of
emotions-manager to their wives. They want to know how their
sons are feeling. They want to share their own feelings with their
children. Not surprisingly, fathers are increasingly being seen by
sons as reliable sources of emotional nurturing. In the future,
even more fathers will refuse to abdicate participation in the
emotional life of the family. It's to be hoped that they will become as emotionally articulate and attuned as their wives.

Emphasis on family and community has generated many
other spinoffs as well:

- Fathers have already begun to broaden their perspective on communication, and men are becoming less hier-
  archy-conscious. An important purpose of communication is now to facilitate interpersonal connections, not
  just to maintain one's position in a hierarchy or to impart information. This revised perspective will become
  even more widespread as more and more men become
  sensitized to the emotional benefits of satisfying interpersonal relationships.

- Fathers and sons already feel more comfortable display-
  ing a range of behaviors that were unavailable to their
  past counterparts. For example, spontaneous and explicit signs of affection are no longer taboo, because men
  are no longer locked into such a limited definition of
  what it means to be a man. This expansion of the be-
  havioral repertoire for males will continue, and will ul-

timately have the effect of deepening and enriching relationships between fathers and sons.

- Fathers and sons are increasingly able to share concerns and provide emotional support for each other. In the future, they will talk even more meaningfully and on many levels.

*Fathers are now able to reveal more of their inner life and emotions.* Until recently, a father's influence has primarily been wielded indirectly, through modeling and metaphor. This has been a way to avoid more direct expression of his inner life. Men now can be more open and direct, more self-disclosing, exerting their paternal influence more directly. This reduces the potential for misunderstanding between fathers and sons, since it requires less guesswork on the son's part. Father is a known quantity, open and human.

It would be wrong to expect that modeling and metaphor will cease to serve as tools which fathers use to influence their sons. These tools will continue to be used. But they will be supplemented by talk.

As a related consequence, fathers in the future will rely less heavily on criticism—offering correction and advice—as a way of influencing their sons. With more open lines of communication, the influence they exert can be more positive and direct.

*The long-standing tie between achievement, identity, and self-worth has begun to be loosened.* Life is seen by contemporary men less as a battle than a journey, with ample opportunities for wonder and joy along the way.

This trend will gain momentum, further reducing the pressure on men to perform. The problems that now affect so many of them in the workplace and in intimate relationships will gradually diminish. For example, success obsession will be reduced, as will emotional remoteness from family.

## Demographic Changes

Value shifts aside, changing demographics have forced men into roles that are different from the ones they played before.

With the sharp increase in two-income families, as well as the ease of divorce, more men than ever before are being called to serve as primary caretaker at least some of the time. In an increasing number of cases, single men are learning to be primary caretakers all the time.

### Two-Income Families

The data are compelling. Two-income families are on the rise, comprising nearly 56.2 percent of all families in 1987, and 57.6 percent in 1990. In such families, fathers assume responsibility as primary caretakers at least some of the time. It's no longer unusual to see a man pushing a stroller or with a baby in a backpack, alone with his children at the park, in shopping malls, or in the grocery store.

### Divorce and Custodial Fathers

In 1965, approximately 26 percent of all marriages ended in divorce. By 1981 the figure was approximately 50 percent of all marriages. Though much has been made of a lowering of the divorce rate to 49.5 percent in 1990, demographers are yet to arrive at a definitive interpretation of these data. (The fact that more couples than ever are having children out of wedlock needs to be factored into these statistics.)

Until recently, it was automatically assumed that when divorce occurred, the mother would be awarded custody. (Only a decade ago 10.8 million of the 12 million American children of divorce were  in their mother's custody.) Contributing to this was a widely believed myth that while father could be a good breadwinner and protector, he lacked the ability, purely on the basis of gender, to nurture and care for children.

Research has shattered that myth. It's become clear that men are, indeed, effective nurturers. Kyle Pruett, a psychiatrist who conducted a long-term study of men as primary caretakers, reports that, although a man's manner of dealing with children is not the same as a woman's, it is in all respects entirely satisfactory. Children of both genders raised primarily or exclusively by fathers display many desirable characteristics, among them advanced social skills and an unusually well-developed ability to cope with a highly stimulating environment. They certainly are none the worse for having been cared for much of the time by a man.

Such findings, along with the cultural changes discussed earlier, have caused the courts and state legislatures to rethink untested assumptions about child custody. More men than ever are seeking and winning joint custody. (At last report, 30 states had legislation on the books authorizing such arrangements.) Other men are seeking and being awarded sole custody.

The number of single-parent families headed by men has been growing steadily for years. In 1987, the figure was only 13.2 percent. By 1992, it had increased to 15 percent, or more than 1.4 million families. When these single-parent families are created as a result of a divorce agreement, as approximately two-thirds of them are, that decision is only sometimes based on the court's decision that the mother is unfit to be the custodial parent. Said one custodial father I spoke with, "I never really questioned my ex-wife's ability to be an adequate parent. I just knew I'd be better."

So many more fathers than ever before have taken on primary responsibility for childcare, it hardly seems surprising that more of them are getting better at it. Demographic changes are forcing changes in the way fathers think about and deal with their offspring. There's been a blurring of the rigid boundaries that once separated maternal and paternal behavior. Fathers and sons can only profit from the change.

### Taking the Long View

There is no guarantee that the many gains in the potential for intimacy between fathers and sons will be maintained. Nor is it certain that positive trends will necessarily continue. Cultural and social evolution is not an automatic or irreversible process: change is the result of insight, effort, and a willingness to take risks. If the members of a culture stop learning, growing, and exerting a positive influence, the changes that have begun to come about will be lost. Not only will progress come to a halt, there's also a strong likelihood that regression will occur. (The growth of the neo-Nazi party in the 1990s is a grim warning that not all social movement is progressive.)

You fashion your world through the choices you make for yourself as an individual. You create yourself and you also create your community. Rather than be the victim of your culture, you can mold it into a better, more serviceable form.

No matter what your past was, you have the freedom to make changes. Perhaps this book has given you some food for thought about the sorts of changes you'd like to see in yourself, your relationships, and society.

Both sexes stand to gain by taking responsibility for the human community we all shape. Women's liberation and men's liberation are complementary in both spirit and effect. Only the foolish on both sides see men's and women's interests as antithetical. Although it's certainly true that women have been victimized by our culture, so have men. Only by cooperating can the two sexes create a more humane world and simultaneously eliminate victimization on both sides.

Something else must be remembered about the evolution of the father-son relationship: nothing can be changed completely in one or even two generations. Concerted effort over many lifetimes will be required for the seeds that have begun to sprout to take root and become established. What fathers do in dealing with their sons today determines the kinds of fathers their sons will become in turn. The impact of your decisions today will reach far into the future.

# Recommended Reading

Fanning, P., and M. McKay (1993) *Being a Man: A Guide to the New Masculinity*. Oakland, CA: New Harbinger Publications, Inc.

Keen, S. (1991) *Fire in the Belly: On Being a Man*. New York: Bantam Books.

Pruett, K. (1987) *The Nurturing Father*. New York: Warner Books.

Vogt, G. M., and S. T. Stirridge (1992) *Like Son, Like Father*. New York: Plenum Press.

# Other New Harbinger Self-Help Titles

*Father-Son Healing: An Adult Son's Guide*, $12.95
*The Chemotherapy Survival Guide*, $11.95
*Your Family/Your Self: How to Analyze Your Family System*, $11.95
*Being a Man: A Guide to the New Masculinity*, $12.95
*The Deadly Diet, Second Edition: Recovering from Anorexia & Bulimia*, $11.95
*Last Touch: Preparing for a Parent's Death*, $11.95
*Consuming Passions: Help for Compulsive Shoppers*, $11.95
*Self-Esteem, Second Edition*, $12.95
*Depression & Anxiety Mangement: An audio tape for managing emotional problems*, $11.95
*I Can't Get Over It, A Handbook for Trauma Survivors*, $12.95
*Concerned Intervention, When Your Loved One Won't Quit Alcohol or Drugs*, $11.95
*Redefining Mr. Right*, $11.95
*Dying of Embarrassment: Help for Social Anxiety and Social Phobia*, $11.95
*The Depression Workbook: Living With Depression and Manic Depression*, $13.95
*Risk-Taking for Personal Growth: A Step-by-Step Workbook*, $11.95
*The Marriage Bed: Renewing Love, Friendship, Trust, and Romance*, $11.95
*Focal Group Psychotherapy: For Mental Health Professionals*, $44.95
*Hot Water Therapy: Save Your Back, Neck & Shoulders in 10 Minutes a Day* $11.95
*Older & Wiser: A Workbook for Coping With Aging*, $12.95
*Prisoners of Belief: Exposing & Changing Beliefs that Control Your Life*, $10.95
*Be Sick Well: A Healthy Approach to Chronic Illness*, $11.95
*Men & Grief: A Guide for Men Surviving the Death of a Loved One.*, $11.95
*When the Bough Breaks: A Helping Guide for Parents of Sexually Abused Childern*, $11.95
*Love Addiction: A Guide to Emotional Independence*, $11.95
*When Once Is Not Enough: Help for Obsessive Compulsives*, $11.95
*The New Three Minute Meditator*, $9.95
*Getting to Sleep*, $10.95
*The Relaxation & Stress Reduction Workbook, 3rd Edition*, $13.95
*Leader's Guide to the Relaxation & Stress Reduction Workbook*, $19.95
*Beyond Grief: A Guide for Recovering from the Death of a Loved One*, $10.95
*Thoughts & Feelings: The Art of Cognitive Stress Intervention*, $13.95
*Messages: The Communication Skills Book*, $12.95
*The Divorce Book*, $11.95
*Hypnosis for Change: A Manual of Proven Techniques, 2nd Edition*, $12.95
*The Chronic Pain Control Workbook*, $13.95
*Rekindling Desire: Bringing Your Sexual Relationship Back to Life*, $12.95
*Visualization for Change*, $12.95
*Videotape: Clinical Hypnosis for Stress & Anxiety Reduction*, $24.95
*Starting Out Right: Essential Parenting Skills for Your Child's First Seven Years*, $12.95
*Big Kids: A Parents' Guide to Weight Control for Children*, $11.95
*My Parent's Keeper: Adult Children of the Emotionally Disturbed*, $11.95
*When Anger Hurts*, $12.95
*Free of the Shadows: Recovering from Sexual Violence*, $12.95
*Lifetime Weight Control*, $11.95
*The Anxiety & Phobia Workbook*, $13.95
*Love and Renewal: A Couple's Guide to Commitment*, $12.95
*The Habit Control Workbook*, $12.95

Call **toll free, 1-800-748-6273,** to order. Have your Visa or Mastercard number ready. Or send a check for the titles you want to New Harbinger Publications, Inc., 5674 Shattuck Avenue, Oakland, CA 94609. Include $2.00 for the first book and 50¢ for each additional book, to cover shipping and handling. (California residents please include appropriate sales tax.) Allow four to six weeks for delivery.

*Prices subject to change without notice.*